1000
Hints & Tips
for Better Digital
Photos & Videos

Design: Fineline Studios
Art Director: Tony Seddon
Compiled and updated by Steve Luck

Fall River Press
122 Fifth Avenue
New York, NY 10011

ISBN: 978-1-4351-1634-4

Printed and bound in Singapore by Star Standard Industries (Pte) Ltd.

10 9 8 7 6 5 4 3 2 1

1000
Hints & Tips
for Better Digital
Photos & Videos

Philip Andrews, Jamie Ewbank,
Lee Frost, Rob Hull, & Chris Weston

FALL
RIVER
PRESS

Contents

Equipment

Capture

Image Editing

Output

Digital Video

Video Editing

Introduction

In much the same way that the invention of the Kodak Brownie box camera opened up photography to the masses, the advent of digital capture technology has developed a whole new generation of photo enthusiasts. Rather than taking photography away from its roots, digital capture offers us far greater control over our images than ever before.

Although digital capture technology has been revolutionary, the practice of photography really hasn't changed at all. Great pictures still require that you understand the basic principles of photography–light, composition, design, creativity, and vision–and no amount of computer manipulation will produce a compelling picture from a poorly constructed array of pixels.

So how does digital photography work? In principle, it works much the same way as traditional film photography. Light passes through a lens onto a light-sensitive material, which absorbs and amplifies the light in order to make it visible. Previously, this material was a piece of film, but it has been replaced in digital photography by an electronic digital photosensor (DPS).

This sensor is an array of millions of light-sensitive cells, or photodiodes (PD), each responding to an amount of light falling on it when the camera's shutter is opened to expose it. A corresponding signal is then created, which in turn is digitized (given a number value) so that a computer can read it.

One major advantage of digital photography is that you can shoot and preview as you go. Other advantages include:

- Better results, more often: Instant picture feedback allows you to make immediate adjustments to camera settings and composition

- Control: With digital cameras you have far greater control over the final image than you've ever had with film. No more relying on poor-quality stores for your shots.

- Image quality: A bit controversial, but, compared to like-for-like 35mm cameras, sensors are superior at picking out detail, particularly in low-light conditions.

- Flexibility: The number of things you can do with your photographs once they're turned into digital code is amazing. Websites, greetings cards, DVDs, calendars, and fine-art prints are all within range.

This handy volume walks you through some of the techniques you'll need in your everyday photography, as well as insights, tips, and advice for photographing sport and action, vacation and travel, products, and in night and low light conditions, to name a few. Some of the hints and tips will inspire you to think in new ways and to see apparent obstacles as well as opportunities, while others offer advice about good photography practice and maintaining and packing your gear. This book also looks at image processing and editing, and ways to improve the appearance of your photographs post-capture.

As with digital photography, digital video technology provides the opportunity to make a record of something precious, and videomaking in the twenty first century offers much more than just a collection of images. Like digital photography, videomaking is not simply a case of recording on your camcorder and then putting it on videotape for others to see—there are a diverse number of ways for your family, friends, and even unsuspecting members of the general public to view what you've done.

Computers, software packages, disc burners, and the Internet have paved the way for sharing your precious, funny, dramatic, and poignant home videos. There is a wide selection of easy-to-use and affordable software to edit out the moments you don't want in your videos, and then burn a movie onto disc. You can even put your movies on the Internet or send them via email.

This book presents 1000 hints, tips, and techniques that will get you taking pictures and video like a pro. From choosing the right equipment through to digital editing and making prints, this book will show you how. What you'll find is simple to understand, easy to implement, proven advice for quick results. This is a book that you can dip into as your knowledge grows, and learn something new every time that you do.

GALLERY—TAKE PICTURES WITH IMPACT

GALLERY

Equipment

Compact digital cameras

For general use, such as holiday and family snaps, modern digital compact cameras can produce excellent pictures with perfectly adequate image quality. There is a huge variety of compact point-and-shoot cameras on the market, so before you go out and buy one you need to know how to decipher the manufacturers' and retailers' marketing spiel so that you make the right decision. Here is what to look out for.

001 Pixel count

All digital cameras have a megapixel number–1 megapixel is equal to 1 million pixels. Each pixel represents a site on the camera's sensor where an element of the scene can be recorded or photographed. Therefore, the more megapixels a camera has, the more detail it can record. However, manufacturers use megapixel count as a major marketing tool and often compact camera sensors are crammed with too many megapixels, which can detract from image quality, particularly in low-light conditions. So more megapixels is not necessarily better, particularly if you only want small prints. Read reviews in camera magazines or on websites about the image quality of the cameras on your shortlist.

002 Viewfinder

The viewfinder provides direct viewing of the subject but is offset from the lens, so that what you see through the finder isn't exactly what you get in the final image– this is known as "parallax error." Some sophisticated DSLR-type cameras, have an electronic viewfinder (EVF), which shows exactly the scene that the sensor will capture when the shutter release is pressed. Although not as responsive nor as bright as a DSLR's optical viewfinder, EVFs overcome the parallax error and work well in bright conditions (see Tip 3).

005 Shutter lag

Some digital cameras have a noticeable delay between pressing the shutter release and the camera actually taking the photo. This lag is caused by the camera using precious time to focus the lens and set the exposure, and can make spontaneous photography of moving subjects, such as children, animals, and sport, almost impossible. Shutter lag can be partially avoided by planning in advance where the action is going to happen, half depressing the shutter release so the camera focuses and sets the exposure in advance and then completely depressing the shutter release when the subject comes into view.

003 Viewfinder or LCD?

Because many digital cameras show the scene directly on the LCD (liquid crystal display) screen on the back of the camera, in theory there is no need for a viewfinder. However, using the LCD necessitates holding the camera away from the body for effective viewing. Using a viewfinder makes the camera more stable, as it is held close to the body. A viewfinder is also useful in bright conditions when it is often difficult to see the image on the LCD.

004 Shutter release

In most cameras, the shutter release has two stages. Pressing it halfway activates any AF (autofocus) and AE (autoexposure) functions, which will remain "locked" so long as the button remains depressed. Pressing the shutter release all the way will then activate the shutter and take the picture.

Angle-of-view

The amount a lens actually sees and records depends on its angle of view, which is expressed in degrees. The wider the lens (or lens setting), the bigger its angle of view and vice versa. The 50mm standard focal length lens (or lens setting) has an angle of view similar to the naked eye, while wide-angle lenses (or settings) have an angle of view that's greater, and telephoto lenses (or settings) a smaller one, as shown by the below illustration.

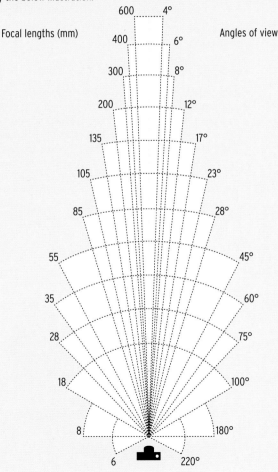

Focal lengths (mm)   Angles of view

600 — 4°
400 — 6°
300 — 8°
200 — 12°
135 — 17°
105 — 23°
85 — 28°
55 — 45°
35 — 60°
28 — 75°
18 — 100°
8 — 180°
6 — 220°

006 Zoom lens

If your camera has a zoom lens, then the zoom control allows you to alter the focal length (magnification factor) of the lens, usually from wide angle (for subjects such as landscapes) to telephoto (essential for wildlife or sport).

007 Magnification factor

Choose a camera with a lens that allows you to best photograph the subjects you're most interested in. For general photography, such as holidays, family events, and landscape scenes, a zoom lens with a magnification of 3x is ideal, while for wildlife and sports, where your subject is usually some distance away, you may prefer a greater magnification—even up to 10x.

008 Optical zoom vs. digital zoom

If you want a camera with a long zoom, go for one with an optical (as opposed to a digital) zoom. A digital zoom works by cropping and then digitally enlarging the central area of the frame, giving the effect of zooming in, but the process significantly decreases image quality so should only be used as a last resort.

009 LCD panel

The LCD panel enables you to review your photographs instantly. This allows you to spot any poor pictures and reshoot.

010 LCD magnification

Options to magnify the image in the LCD are useful, allowing you to check small details of the photograph for sharpness and good composition (for example, making sure your subject didn't blink when the picture was taken).

011 Exposure modes

If you wish to retain some control over exposure, or if you expect your photography to develop beyond simple point-and-shoot, then look for a camera that offers some form of manual exposure override. This may be (at the very least) an exposure compensation (EV) function, or (preferably) aperture-priority and/or shutter priority AE, or full manual exposure.

Flash Tips

012 Flash

Some cameras offer a choice of flash modes that may include:
• red-eye reduction (see tip 014, below)
• flash-on, which provides fill-light on brighter days
• flash-off, for use when flash is prohibited (for example, at some religious festivals, in museums, and at zoos).

013 In-camera flash

The most important aspect to flash is the guide number– a measurement of the power of the flash unit. The more powerful the flash (as denoted by a higher guide number), the farther the light travels. If you want to photograph subjects from a distance, such as in a large sports arena, then choose a camera with a more powerful flash unit.

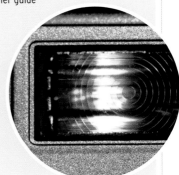

014 Red-eye reduction facility

If you take a lot of photographs of people or animals, then make sure the camera you choose has a red-eye reduction facility, which will help avoid those gruesome demon eyes.

Digital Single Lens Reflex (DSLR) cameras

For better image quality due to larger sensors and greater photodiversity, the digital SLR is the ideal camera for anyone taking their photography seriously. Still relatively lightweight and becoming increasingly affordable, its larger size provides more room for processing power, while the ability to change lenses results in high-quality images of a variety of photo situations, from wide-angle landscapes to close-up action shots—and a whole range of bolt-on accessories is available.

015 Shutter release

Unlike digital compact cameras, DSLRs do not suffer from time lag between pressing the shutter release and the camera taking the photo, making response times much quicker. You're less likely to miss a photo opportunity with a DSLR.

016 Mode selector dial

Most DSLRs provide the photographer with much more creative freedom through the use of manual and semi-automatic shooting modes, which can be easily accessed via a mode selector dial. For less-experienced photographers using a DSLR for the first time, look for an "entry-level" DSLR as these also provide standard shooting modes, such as "landscape," "sports," and "portrait" settings.

017 Lens mount

All DSLRs have their own proprietary lens mount, so Canon DSLRs can only accept lenses made by Canon or by third-party lens manufacturers that make lenses with the Canon lens mount. Similarly Nikon cameras can only accept Nikon lenses (or third-party lenses with a Nikon mount). When choosing a DSLR body, therefore, you should also consider the quality and variety of lenses that will fit the body. You may only start with a standard zoom lens, but as your interest develops you'll want to add to your lens collection.

018 Depth of field preview

Managing lens aperture to govern how much and which specific areas of your potential image are in-focus is one of the fundamental elements of photographic technique. This little button makes life easier by allowing you to preview the available depth of field.

019 AF mode

If you enjoy photographing moving subjects, such as sporting events, wildlife, and candid portraiture, then it's worth investing in a camera that has an AF tracking function, which maintains focus on a moving subject.

020 Viewfinder

Not all cameras have a viewfinder with 100 percent coverage. It's helpful to know what coverage your camera has so that you can allow for the unseen areas of the photograph when defining your composition, realizing that the scene the sensor will capture is more than you see through the viewfinder. Generally only professional DSLRs show 100 percent coverage.

021 Focus points

Murphy's Law has it that your subject is never in the same area of the picture space as your focus points. The more focus points the camera has, the more likely you are not to fall foul of one of AF's main limitations, particularly if your preferred theme is action or sport's photography.

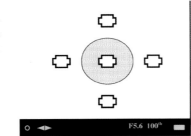

022 Rear LCD panel

Like compact cameras, DSLRs all feature a rear LCD panel that is used for previewing images and navigating through various menus and options. Some DSLR models also feature a live preview function, which allows the photographer to compose the image using the LCD screen as an alternative to the optical viewfinder, this can be particularly helpful for achieving accurate focus when shooting with a macro lens for extreme close-ups.

023 Accessory shoe

If you plan to use on-camera flash and certain remote trigger devices, then your camera will need an accessory shoe.

024 Burst rate

For fast-moving action, you need a camera with a high burst rate. There are two things to look out for: the continuous shooting rate, usually measured in frames per second (fps), and the buffer size. The larger the buffer size, the more images can be taken at full burst rate.

025 ISO rating

The lower the ISO setting (e.g. 100), the more light is required to form an accurately exposed image when compared with a higher ISO rating (e.g. 1600). The greater the ISO range the camera has, the more control you will have over exposure and composition. Because of their larger sensor sizes, most DSLRs are excellent at producing almost noise-free images up to around 800 ISO. The most recent DSLRs offer ISO settings as high as 25,600, although the resulting images are, unsurprisingly, extremely noisy.

026 Build quality

Most of the more affordable cameras are manufactured in molded plastics, suitable for general use but unable to withstand too many hard knocks or continuous heavy use. More expensive cameras often have a metal chassis that helps to protect the precision engineering within. This is worth the additional cost if your camera's likely to undergo some knocks and bumps.

Interchangeable lenses

A DSLR's sensor will only record what it sees through the camera's lens, and no amount of post-production manipulation with a computer will able to generate detail that never existed in the first instance. The lens, more than any other single factor, affects the quality of your final image. Here are some considerations to take into account when choosing lenses.

027 Equivalent focal length

Although an increasing number of DSLRs are equipped with full-frame (35mm) sensors, the vast majority feature APS-C or "cropped" sensors, which are around 30–40 percent smaller than 35mm sensors. Cameras with APS-C sensors tend to be smaller and less expensive, while still providing excellent image quality. One effect of a smaller sensor is that it increases the focal length of the lens by narrowing the angle-of-view. In reality this means that the focal length of a standard 50mm lens, which on a full-frame camera would provide a view close to that of the human eye, is increased by around 50 percent to an equivalent focal length (efl) of 75mm, a short telephoto lens. While this has the benefit of increasing the focal length of zoom lenses, for example, from 200mm to 300mm, it does reduce the wide-angle capability of short focal-length lenses; for example what would have been considered a wide-angle 24mm becomes a more standard 36mm lens. To counter this, and in order to create lenses that work efficiently with sensors, lens manufacturers now produce lenses, such as Canon's EF-S series, which are designed to work specifically with cropped sensors. So bear in mind equivalent focal length when choosing lenses.

028 Cost

Always buy the most expensive lenses you can afford. Choose a less expensive camera body and a quality lens rather than vice versa. It is the lens that passes the information (i.e. light) through to the sensor, which then records it. If the information isn't there to start with, you'll never recreate it on a computer. In addition, good-quality lenses hold their value much better than camera bodies.

029 Prime lenses

Prime lenses (lenses of a fixed focal length) are generally of better optical quality, due mainly to the reduction in the amount of glass through which the light has to pass. For very wide-angle lenses and super telephoto lenses, prime lenses give noticeably better image quality.

030 Zoom lenses

Zoom lenses provide the greatest flexibility in composition, allowing you to alter the focal length exactly as needed–and today's modern zoom lenses provide very good images. However, if you're very discerning about image quality, avoid extreme zooms (those with a very wide range, such as 28–300mm), as their quality is compromised by their versatility.

031 Determining perspective

A lens with an equivalent focal length of 50mm will give you an image that is close to that perceived by the human eye. A wide-angle lens (i.e. efl less than 50mm) will increase the amount of the scene visible in the picture space and make objects within the scene appear further apart. Telephoto lenses, on the other hand, will include less of the scene and make the objects appear to be bigger and closer together.

032 Autofocus

If speed of focusing is important to you, then always test AF performance before you buy any AF lens–some systems are much slower than others.

033 Independent vs. own-brand lenses

While there are some exceptions to the rule, the best own-brand lenses (such as Nikon and Canon) are better quality than the best independents (such as Tamron, Sigma, and Tokina). However, such independent manufacturers do offer less-expensive alternatives, and it is worth reviewing some of the test reports published in photography magazines and on photo websites for specific like-for-like comparisons.

034 IS and VR lenses

Image stabilization (IS) and vibration reduction (VR) lenses utilize internal sensors that detect camera shake and motors that automatically adjust the lens elements to minimize blur. This technology reduces camera shake, and allows handholding of the camera at shutter speeds slower than with a conventional lens. The two systems, developed by Canon and Nikon respectively, are a real bonus when handholding the camera is the only option and pinsharp images are essential.

035 Antishake

An alternative to IS and VR lenses is antishake technology, as employed by Sony in their DSLRs. With this technology the camera picks up movement from your hands and finely adjusts the position of the sensor to compensate and reduce blur.

036 Maximum lens aperture

The maximum aperture of the lens will, to some extent, dictate the level of control you have over exposure settings. For example, in low light conditions with a slow lens (e.g. a lens with a maximum aperture of f/5.6 or less) you may not be able to attain the shutter speed necessary to freeze motion or capture a sharp image. However, with long-telephoto lenses, a wide maximum aperture dictates a very large and heavy lens, which can be difficult to carry and support. When selecting a lens, try to determine beforehand the conditions you are most likely to be photographing in and balance maximum aperture with portability.

037 Maximum aperture and zoom lenses

With some zoom lenses, the maximum aperture can vary depending on the focal length set. This system is used to reduce the size and weight of the lens but, again, can limit your options when it comes to setting exposure. If possible, always opt for a zoom lens with a fixed maximum aperture.

038 Macro lenses

These are used when you want to get very close to the subject, often within inches, and when you want to create lifesize or bigger magnification. They come in varying focal lengths—usually from 50mm to 200mm—as well as a zoom range. Image quality is generally superb, with very minimal levels of distortion.

039 Lens hoods

Lens flare is caused by stray light from the sun, or other light sources, falling directly onto the front of the lens and then bouncing around the inside of the lens barrel. It shows as polygonal shapes on your pictures, which do nothing for composition and artistic merit. Attaching a lens hood to the front of the lens helps to soak up any light and minimizes the effect. It is advisable to always use the lens manufacturer's recommended model, particularly with wide-angle lenses, to avoid vignetting, which can occur if the hood is too large and cuts into the angle-of-view of the lens.

Necessities and accessories

Camera stores offer a multitude of different accessories and gadgets that you can add to your camera system. Some will be of little use to you in reality, while others, such as memory cards, are essential.

Memory cards

One of the main differences between digital and film cameras is the storage media on which all of your images can be stored—this is usually in the form of a removable card. So what are the options and implications of each?

Types of memory device

040 What do memory cards do?

After you take a photograph, the camera converts the light signals into digital data and, depending on the file type, processes the information before transferring it onto a memory device inserted in the camera body. The purpose of the memory device is to provide semipermanent storage of images until they can be downloaded to a computer's hard-disk drive or other form of long-term storage media, such as a DVD or portable hard disk.

041 SmartMedia (SM)

SM is extremely lightweight and wafer-thin, though this makes it quite fragile for use in the field. This format is less popular than it once was, with very few cameras new to the market supporting it.

042 MultiMedia (MMC)

These are designed to interface with an array of digital devices, from cameras to mobile phones, that have either an MMC slot or a Secure Digital (SD) slot. There are two variants to MMC: Secure MMC and Reduced-size MMC.

043 Secure Digital (SD)

These are ultra-lightweight and wafer thin, and although fragile, they do allow for fast data transfer. They feature security functions to protect data and also have a write-protection switch on the side.

044 xD Picture Card

Developed by Olympus, Fujifilm, and Toshiba, the small xD Picture Card format is designed to be used in ultra-compact cameras.

045 Sony Memory Stick

Sony's Memory Sticks are widely used in their digital cameras and video recorders. Compatibility with other makers is poor but reliability and capacity is good. An erasure-protection lock prevents overwriting or deletion of files.

046 Microdrive

IBM's Microdrive is, in effect, a miniature hard-disk drive the same size as a CompactFlash card (see Tip 47). Historically, byte for byte, Microdrives are less expensive than CompactFlash cards, but are less reliable due to their moving parts.

047 CompactFlash (CF)

CF cards are the most popular form of storage media on the market today. Utilizing solid-state technology and being a robust size, they tend to be more reliable than most other formats and usually lead the market in terms of storage capacity. Although capacities of 100GB are available, the most popular sizes range from between 1GB and 16GB, with the smaller storage cards tending to write faster.

048 Type I and Type II cards—what's the difference?

CF cards are available in two physical sizes, referred to as Type I and Type II. Type II cards are thicker. While practically all current digital cameras accept both card types, some earlier models accept only the thinner Type I device.

049 Write-speed

Write-speeds range from about 10x to more than 100x. The quicker the write-speed, the faster the data is transferred from the camera's internal memory to the card, which can increase burst-depth. Faster cards tend to be more expensive, so consider whether the type of photography you most enjoy warrants fast write-speed cards.

Transfer Speeds for CF Cards

Card speed	Data-transfer speed (MB/second)
8x	1.2
12x	1.8
20x	3.0
25x	3.8
30x	4.5
40x	6.0
60x	9.0
66x	10.0
80x	12.0

050 Capacity—is there an ideal?

With capacity increasing all the time, this question boils down to two main issues: manageability and reliability. With a 12-megapixel DSLR, it is possible to store more than 1,000 images on an 8GB memory card (depending on the file type). If the card were to fail or become lost, that's a lot of photographs to lose. Your decision may also be influenced by the type of photography you do. For example, when photographing action, such as sports or wildlife, you may find that switching cards is inconvenient and that higher-capacity cards enable fewer card changeovers. This may be less of an issue for less time-sensitive subjects, such as still life and studio photography.

052 Deleting files from the memory card

You can erase unwanted images from the memory card as you go along, freeing capacity. The only time you shouldn't remove the card from a camera or other device is when the camera's computer is accessing the card. Always refer to the Access Indicator lights to tell you if it is safe to remove the card.

051 Using memory cards

The first time you use a new memory card, you should format it, which is usually done via a camera menu option (refer to your user guide).

053 Taking memory cards through airport X-ray machines

Unlike film, memory cards are unaffected by the X-ray machines used for checking hand luggage and the more powerful ones used by airport authorities to scan baggage placed in the hold.

Mobile storage devices

Out in the field it is useful to be able to transfer your files from memory cards to a more permanent form of storage. This frees up space on the memory card to let you take more pictures; it protects photographs from accidental loss or damage, and it provides a reliable backup until you get home and download the images to your computer.

054 Portable HDD

Portable HDD (hard-disk drives) provide pocket-sized storage of up to some 40GB of data, which equates to hundreds or even thousands of digital images. They generally have a screen for previewing images and the stored files can be transferred to a computer, or sent to a printer to make prints.

055 Portable CD writers

These work by writing the information from the memory card to the CD-R or CD-RW disc, which means you need to carry some spare discs with you. There is no facility for viewing images, which must be transferred to a PC or Mac for viewing.

056 Reliability

The single-most vulnerable part of any computer is the HDD. This is because it is the only mechanical component. HDDs don't like being moved and jolted around, which can lead to faults occurring. A CD, on the other hand, once written, is relatively immune to damage and so provides a more stable medium for portable storage.

057 Backup files

The other advantage of the CD over the HDD is backup. Once the CD is written, it can be retained as a permanent backup to your computer storage in case your computer should fail at any time.

058 Card compatibility

When choosing a portable storage device make sure that it accepts the memory card type you are using.

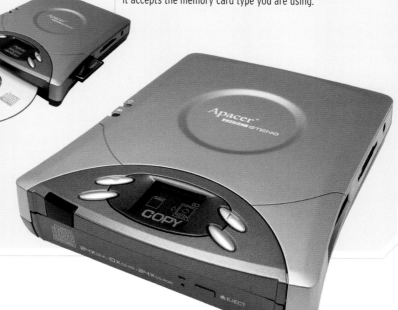

Carrying your equipment

If you're keen on your photography hobby, you will soon build up a good deal of equipment to carry when you are out and about. There are numerous options for carrying equipment in the field, and often what's right is what you find most comfortable.

059 Hard cases

A hard case is ideal for carrying equipment safely on an airplane. Watertight and airtight, hard cases withstand the roughest treatment from airline baggage handlers. They are, however, very heavy and often quite cumbersome, though the better ones have wheels to make them more portable.

060 Backpacks

These are similar to the type of pack you would use for outdoor activities, except that the inside has dividers to store and protect equipment. Backpacks are ideal for adventurous outdoor photographers who carry large amounts of equipment for relatively long periods. They vary in price, but you should expect to pay a lot for a good one.

061 Pouches

If you just want to carry a single camera with you then a belt pouch is a simple, comfortable means of keeping your camera safe and accessible.

062 Rucksacks

There are an increasing number of bags on the market that resemble rucksacks, and which are capable of carrying a DSLR, 3-4 lenses, and other accessories. Lowepro, for example, manufacture a range of rucksacks that can be quickly twisted around the body so that your camera gear is readily accessible.

063 Handbags

If you're carrying a relatively small amount of equipment and not traveling far, a handbag may be the best choice. These come in various sizes and will carry a complete SLR system, including a selection of lenses. Side pockets offer useful additional storage space for small accessories such as a remote shutter release and small flash units.

064 Size

Make sure the bag or case has enough room to carry all the equipment you might need at any one time, plus some room for any new equipment you may end up buying at a later date.

065 Weight

Make sure the bag is light enough when full for you to carry it for long periods, if, for example, you are interested in landscape or wildlife photography.

066 Carrying tripods

If you regularly use a tripod, choose a bag that offers a built-in tripod carrier. This will make your life much easier on those daylong treks and hikes through the countryside.

067 Padding

As well as being convenient, a camera bag should offer adequate protection for your expensive and delicate equipment. Make sure that the bag you choose has good, firm padding that will absorb any bumps and knocks.

068 Accessibility

Make sure your equipment is easy to locate and access from the bag. There's nothing worse than rummaging around in a disorganized pack while some extraordinary event occurs in front of you.

069 Airlines

Give airline staff your every assistance. If possible, carry your delicate gear (cameras, lenses, laptop, etc.) as cabin baggage. If you have too much equipment, use a photo-specific hard case, and check it in as hold baggage.

070 Security

If you check in a camera bag with the airline, place it in an old duffel bag, or disguise it in some other way. A camera bag that looks like what it is is an obvious target for airport thieves.

071 Weather proofing

For outdoor use, get a photo-bag that offers weather protection. Many backpack-type camera bags have a rain resistant cover that can be easily pulled over the case; alternatively, fully waterproof bags are also available.

072 Comfort

If you opt for a backpack, try it before you buy. Having the adjustable straps fitted specifically for you can make a huge difference. Get the store assistant to help and remember it will weigh more when full.

Camera supports

Keeping your camera steady–and your photographs free of camera shake–is vital. When the light is low, or you're using heavy equipment such as a long telephoto lens, or whenever pin-sharp images are critical, you'll need to use a camera support. Usually, this means a tripod.

073 Tripods

Tripods are the ideal solution to blur-free images. They can be a bit bulky and heavy to carry but they're worth their weight in gold to the serious photographer.

074 Rigidity

Go for the biggest, heaviest tripod you can carry and can afford to buy. The stronger the tripod, the more stable the camera and the better your pictures will be, particularly when you are photographing at slow shutter speeds.

075 Flexibility

For some areas of photography, particularly close-up work, it's useful to have a tripod that is fully flexible, allowing you to get close to the ground and into contorted angles.

076 Carbon fiber

To cut down on weight without compromising rigidity, opt for a carbon fiber tripod. Typically, these are one third lighter than traditional metal tripods, although you can expect to pay a third or more for them.

077 Tripod heads

The tripod head is just as important as the legs. Make sure the model you choose can take the full weight of your camera with your heaviest lens attached, otherwise you'll defeat the object of using the tripod in the first place.

078 Quick release

For speed of operation, choose a tripod head with a quick-release mechanism and always keep a quick-release plate attached to your camera bodies, lenses, and other frequently used equipment. This will save you missing great shots as you unscrew the camera from the bracket.

079 Monopods

A monopod is one solution to the weight and bulk problem of tripods. However, monopods don't offer the same level of sturdiness that a tripod provides.

Flash units

To record an image on a digital sensor you need light. Unfortunately, sometimes there just isn't enough of it. Whether in a dimly lit room or in the low light of dusk or predawn, it's sometimes necessary to add in a little extra light, even with today's highly sensitive DSLRs.

080 Built-in flash

Many DSLRs have a built-in flash that pops up either automatically or when requested depending on the camera's settings. These small flash units are of limited use because of low power and slow recycling times and their position close to the lens gives the least dynamic lighting. However, they can be useful for bursts of fill-flash or when there simply is no alternative. If your DSLR doesn't have a pop-up flash, you'll need a dedicated flash unit if you need extra light.

081 On-camera flash

All DSLRs have an accessory shoe that sits on top of the viewfinder prism, which can be used to hold a dedicated auto-flash unit. These units are more powerful than the built-in variety but suffer the same limitations of flat, frontal lighting. Some units are designed to overcome this problem by letting you angle and/or rotate the flash head for bounce flash, which is much softer in quality than direct, head-on flash.

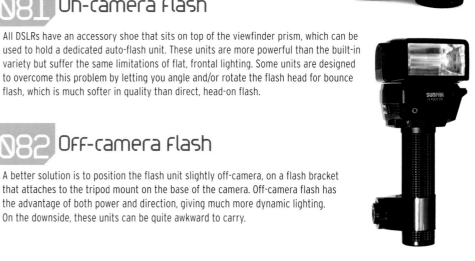

082 Off-camera flash

A better solution is to position the flash unit slightly off-camera, on a flash bracket that attaches to the tripod mount on the base of the camera. Off-camera flash has the advantage of both power and direction, giving much more dynamic lighting. On the downside, these units can be quite awkward to carry.

083 Hammerhead flash

Hammerhead flashes are the most powerful, have the greatest range and quickest recycling times, and are designed to work off-camera. They consist of a large flash head mounted on a stem that doubles as a handle. Although they are less portable than the smaller external units, a wide choice of accessories greatly increases the possibilities for practical application in the field.

084 Diffusers

Diffusers increase the relative size of the light source, similarly creating a soft quality light from a direct light source. Diffusers can be a simple, translucent plastic cover that fits directly over the flash head, or a larger, more sophisticated gadget, resembling a scaled-down version of a softbox.

085 Ring (macro) flash

A special type of flash unit is the ring flash, or macro flash, as it is sometimes referred to because it is used extensively in close-up (macro) photography. This unit fits around the lens barrel and gives shadow-free lighting that can be used to good effect for portraiture as well as macro work. These flashes are quite costly, however, and are limited to specialist use.

What to look for in a flash

086 Power output

In general, the more powerful the flash unit, the greater the control you have over exposure settings and composition. The power is measured by Guide Number (GN): the higher the GN, the more powerful the flash.

087 Coverage

Most flash units are designed to cover an area roughly equivalent to that of the human eye, or an efl 50mm "standard" lens. If you are using a lens with a narrower or wider angle-of-view then the standard flash coverage will either give, respectively, too much or too little light. The best flash units have a zoom function that lets you set the flash coverage to match your lens.

088 Flash exposure compensation

Too much power from the flash unit can overexpose your photographs, for example, when photographing very close to your subject or when using flash for fill-in lighting. Look for a flash unit that lets you reduce the power output for individual shots. Alternatively, most DSLRs allow you reduce the power of the flash via menus on the camera itself.

089 Comparing like for like

When comparing the GN of two or more flash units, check that they have been calculated from the same parameters. For example, a flash unit with a GN of 120 for ISO 1600 equivalency is less powerful than a flash unit with a GN of 40 for ISO 100 equivalency. This is a common marketing technique to make the less powerful flash units appear to be more powerful than they actually are.

090 Flash/camera communication

Manually calculating flash output and exposure can be tedious and takes time. If you want your camera and flash to cope with this, opt for a dedicated flash unit that will "talk" with your camera to make all the necessary exposure decisions, leaving you time to concentrate on composition and framing.

091 Recycling time

If you photograph fast-moving subjects with flash (children, for example), then you will want a flash unit that works in continuous bursts to match your camera. Check what the recycling time of your preferred flash unit is, to make sure it meets your needs.

092 Red-eye reduction

If your camera has a built-in flash unit, check to see whether it also has a red-eye reduction facility and set this to "on" when photographing people or animals. It will help avoid those devil-like eyes caused by light reflecting off the retina.

Filters

Other accessories that you should consider adding to your range of equipment are filters. There are two types of filter—technical filters and creative filters. Technical filters include polarizing and neutral density filters, which are used to enhance or alter the amount of light reaching the sensor, often something that can't be recreated on a computer later. Creative filters, such as the various color or starburst filters, are used to create specific effects, but are rarely used these days as it's often easier to experiment with post-production techniques.

093 Screw-in Filters

Some filters screw onto the front of the lens while others use a filter holder. For the screw-in variety, the lens needs a filter thread, which is often not the case with compact cameras. Filter systems work by attaching a filter holder to the camera, either via the lens or via the tripod mount. Into this you slide the square or rectangular filters. The advantage of this type of system is that one filter will fit all your lenses, whereas with screw-in filters if your lenses have a different front diameter then you'll need another filter to fit.

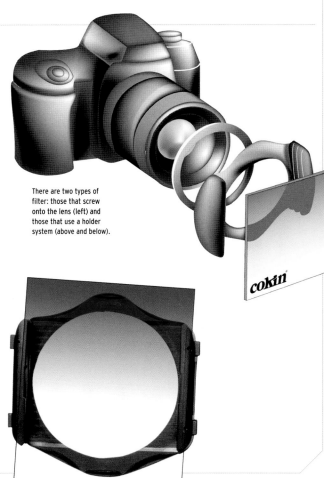

There are two types of filter: those that screw onto the lens (left) and those that use a holder system (above and below).

094 Buy big

Filters themselves come in different sizes, often referred to as "amateur," which are smaller, and the larger and slightly more expensive "professional." I recommend going with the larger size system straight away as it won't be long before you find that amateur filters are too small for some of your lenses—particularly very wide-angle and long telephoto lenses, and some extreme zooms.

095 Ultraviolet (UV)

UV filters remove the invisible ultraviolet light that we can't see but that cameras record. They filter out atmospheric haze in landscape pictures, particularly if taken at altitude, e.g. from an airplane or high up on a mountain. Some photographers keep them on at all times because the filter (which is relatively cheap) protects the (expensive) lens from dirt or damage.

UV filters are useful at high altitude.

096 Neutral density (ND)

ND filters work by reducing the amount of light entering the lens without changing the color cast. They are particularly useful in very bright conditions when, for compositional reasons, you want to use a larger aperture than the prevailing light level would otherwise allow (e.g. to reduce depth of field) or a slower shutter speed (e.g. to blur motion).

097 Polarizing filters

These filters polarize the light entering the lens. They:
• remove the unwanted reflections from shiny non-metallic surfaces, such as water and glass
• darken blue skies and make white clouds more prominent
• can be used to good effect on foliage, which reflects non-polarized light, particularly when wet
• will intensify the color of glossy objects, such as glazed ceramic tiles and shiny plastics.

098 Neutral density graduated (NDG)

This is a variation on the straight ND filter. With an NDG filter, the tone darkens gradually from clear to full strength across the filter. This is useful when one part of the scene is much brighter than another—for example, in a landscape where the sky is very bright and the foreground is in dark shadow. Placing the ND (dark) part of the filter over the sky area reduces the amount of light entering the lens from that part, evening up the tones between the sky and the dark foreground so that your exposure is easier to manage.

Polarizing filters can be used to saturate colors.

NDG filters will even out areas of light and shade.

099 ND & NDG filter strength

These filters come in different strengths, measured in stops. So, if you wanted to reduce your exposure by one stop, for instance, then you would use a one-stop ND or NDG filter. The table (right) lists each filter and its equivalent strength.

Filter	Stops
.3	1
.45	1.5
.6	2
.75	2.5
.9	3

Capture

Exposure basics

Good exposure is the foundation that underpins professional-looking photographs. Although you can fix many problems later in your editing software, it is far better to learn how to capture well-exposed images in-camera than to waste time correcting your mistakes! Here are some tips to help you understand the basics of good exposure.

100 Learn how exposure works

The mechanics of creating a photograph are based on controlling the amount of light entering the camera and, in the case of digital photography, falling on the sensor. This process is called exposing the sensor. All cameras have mechanisms designed to help ensure that just the right amount of light enters the camera. Too much light, and the image will appear washed out (overexposed). Too little, and the picture will be muddy (underexposed).

Increase exposure

101 Controlling exposure

Two different camera parts are used to control the amount of light entering the camera: the aperture and the shutter. It is useful to learn how to use these two essential photographic tools.

102 Learn how the aperture works

The aperture is a variable opening in the camera between the body and the lens. The smaller the hole, the less light is able to enter the camera via the lens. Conversely, if the hole is larger, more light can enter. The variable size of the opening is described in terms of f-numbers or "stops." Confusingly, the smaller the f-number, the larger the hole. It may help to think of the aperture as being similar to your eye's iris. In bright light, the iris is small, restricting the light entering the eye. In dark situations, the iris grows larger to let in more light. So, increase the size of the aperture to lighten the photograph, decrease it to darken.

103 Learn how the shutter works

The shutter works like a roller blind in a window—but at much higher speed! Opening it lets light into the camera, and closing it prevents light from entering. The length of time that the camera's shutter is open, called the shutter speed, determines the amount of light that enters the camera. Fast shutter speeds are used when photographing bright scenes to restrict the light coming into the camera, whereas slow shutter speeds (longer exposures) are used for nighttime or indoor photography. Faster shutter speeds are represented by a series of numbers that are fractions of a second. Slower speeds are displayed in whole seconds.

Decrease exposure

A slow shutter speed creates a feeling of movement in your images.

104 Which shutter and aperture settings?

All cameras have a built-in metering system designed to measure the amount of light entering the camera. The camera uses this measurement as a basis for setting the correct shutter and aperture. Simple cameras use an autoexposure (AE) system that performs this function without the photographer being aware it is happening. More sophisticated models include manual override options. These allow you to take more control over the exposure process, selecting shutter speed and aperture.

105 Sometimes the camera gets it wrong

For perhaps 85 percent of the time, there may be no need to disagree with the camera's meter or the settings that it uses, but there are occasions when the camera can be fooled. It is on these occasions when you need to anticipate the problem and take control. To ensure that you always obtain the best exposure, use the following guidelines.

Better exposure guidelines

106 Use the camera as a guide

The metering system in your camera is very sophisticated and, for the most part, your camera will choose the right exposure settings. All but the most basic models allow you to see shutter and aperture settings in the viewfinder or on the LCD screen. Take a mental note of these and learn to recognize how your camera reacts to different light.

107 Fill the frame with your subject

Most meters use a subject in the center of the frame as a guide for the exposure of the whole image. One way to ensure that your image is well exposed is to make sure that the most important parts of the picture feature in the center of the frame, by which the camera calculates exposure. That said, be wary of monotonous compositions.

108 Use exposure and focus lock

You may wish to try designing the frame with your subject a little off-center. Doing this may help the look of your images, but your exposures might suffer. To solve this, it is helpful to know that most cameras have the ability to lock exposure (and focus) by pushing the shutter button halfway. For the situation where you want to create an off-center shot, point your camera at the subject and press the button halfway and then, without removing your finger, recompose the picture before firing the shutter fully.

109 Create your own reference guide

Assuming you have a manual override on your camera that allows you to set shutter speed and aperture, here's a simple but useful idea for creating your own reference system. Take a series of photographs of a friend in the same location, each time holding a card that has the shutter speed and aperture of the image written on it (along with other details, such as the ISO setting). Repeat the same exercise in different lighting conditions and at different focal lengths. Create an album on your desktop that contains all of these reference images and you'll soon learn what effect each combination of settings has simply by referring to the image.

110 Watch out for darker subjects

The camera's meter works on averages. When you point your lens at a scene, the meter averages the various colors, tones, and brightnesses in the scene to a theoretical mid-gray. The shutter speed and aperture recommended by the camera is based on analyzing how to reproduce this mid-gray in the available lighting conditions. In some circumstances this just doesn't work–for example, in a shot that contains mostly dark subjects. Here, the camera will suggest settings that will result in the picture being overexposed. To compensate, simply increase your shutter speed setting by one or two stops, or close down your aperture by a couple of stops. Preview your results and reshoot if necessary.

111 Keep an eye on light-colored scenes

You should be wary of light-colored scenes for the same reason. Some prime examples are images of beaches or snow. Most pictures in these environments contain large light-colored areas. Leave the camera to its own devices and you will end up with muddy, underexposed pictures. The solution is to add more exposure than the camera recommends. You can do this manually as detailed before, or try using your camera's Exposure Compensation feature. Usually labeled with a small plus and minus sign, this allows you to add or subtract exposure by pressing and turning the command dial. The change in exposure is expressed in fractions of f-stops. For beach and snow scenes, add up to two stops (try 1 or 1.5) and preview.

112 Be careful of backlighting

A portrait taken in front of an open window with a beautiful vista in the distance sounds like a recipe for a stunning photograph, but often the results are not what we expect. The person appears too dark and in some cases is even a silhouette. Assuming this wasn't your intention, your meter has been fooled. The light streaming in the window and surrounding the sitter has made the meter to recommend using a shutter speed and aperture that causes the image to be underexposed. To rectify this, increase the amount of light entering the camera either manually, or with your camera's exposure compensation feature. Shoot the portrait again and preview the results onscreen.

113 Histograms to the rescue!

Being able to preview your work immediately means that many of the exposure mistakes made during the days when film was king can be avoided. Any under- or overexposure problems can be compensated for on the spot and the image reshot. But you need not stop there. Many cameras also contain a built-in graphing function that can display the spread of tones in your image. This graph, usually called a histogram, can be used to diagnose exposure problems quickly and easily. A bump of pixels to the right-hand end of the graph means an underexposed picture, while a bump to the left end indicates overexposure.

Exposure compensation, bracketing, and fill flash

Good exposure is one of the cornerstones of great imaging, and there are numerous techniques you can master to ensure that you capture as much information as possible in your images and get the best possible results from your photography.

114 What characterizes poor exposure?

As we've discussed, images that result from the sensor receiving too much light are overexposed. The indications are that they typically have little or no details in the highlight portions of the image and the midtones are too bright. Underexposed images characteristically lose details in the shadow regions and their midtones are dark.

116 Using exposure compensation (EV)

This control effectively changes the shutter speed or aperture selected in steps of one-third of an f-stop (sometimes also called EV-exposure value). The value increases or decreases the exposure set by the camera in situations when the camera incorrectly reads the scene. Most cameras allow changes of up to plus or minus 3 stops. In tricky lighting scenarios, shoot a test image, preview, adjust, and reshoot.

115 What is perfect exposure?

The perfect exposure will produce a picture that contains:
· A good spread of tones from light to dark
· Details in the shadow areas
· Details in the highlight areas

117 When to use compensation

Don't be overzealous in your quest to produce the perfect exposure, however. Sometimes you can create stunning images by deliberately playing with the exposure—such as so-called "high-key" portraits, where skin tones are fairly bleached out but dark tones might still be rich and detailed. One way to achieve this is to use a very fast ISO setting and add a little exposure compensation. Experiment and see.

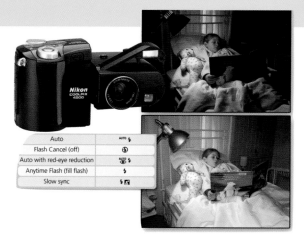

118 Using Fill Flash

A popup flash system provides another way of modifying the spread of tones in your image. In high-contrast circumstances, a little fill flash can help lighten impenetrable shadow areas that would otherwise show no detail.

Auto	AUTO ⚡
Flash Cancel (off)	🚫
Auto with red-eye reduction	AUTO👁 ⚡
Anytime Flash (fill flash)	⚡
Slow sync	⚡🌄

119 Autoexposure Bracketing

For those of you who hate the idea of having to readjust the camera each time you want to make a series of exposure compensations, the Autoexposure Bracketing function might be just what you need. This shoots a sequence of frames with different exposure settings. You can choose between a series of three or five shots and variations in exposure of up to + 2 or - 2 stops. This produces a range of photos from dark to light from which you can select the best result—useful when the camera might have difficulty determining exposure.

Option	No. of shots	Exposure increment	Bracketing order
3, ±0.3	3	±¹/₃ EV	+0.3, 0, −0.3
3, ±0.7	3	±²/₃ EV	+0.7, 0, −0.7
3, ±1.0	3	±1 EV	+1.0, 0, −1.0
5, ±0.3	5	±¹/₃ EV	+0.7, +0.3, 0, −0.3, −0.7
5, ±0.7	5	±²/₃ EV	+1.3, +0.7, 0, −0.7, −1.3
5, ±1.0	5	±1 EV	+2.0, +1.0, 0, −1.0, −2.0

120 Balancing Flash and daylight

Gone are the days when using flash with existing light meant working out complicated ratios and measuring the subject-to-camera distance. Now most cameras contain sophisticated exposure systems that can balance both the ambient light (the existing light already in the scene) and the flash light so that the picture is not overexposed.

121 Correcting Fill-Flash problems

The fill-flash option is another auto function that works well for most scenarios, but there are some instances when you may want a little more control of the flash output. For these occasions, the manufacturers have merged the fill flash and exposure compensation technologies to produce a feature that allows you to adjust the output of the flash independent of the main camera exposure.

122 Flash exposure compensation

The Flash Exposure Compensation feature provides one-third-of-a-stop adjustments for the flash output. Increasing the fill flash's power will mean that it becomes the main light source in the image; reducing the flash power will have the reverse effect so that the existing light dominates and the flash subtly fills the shadows. Use this to adjust the strength of flash in your picture.

Focus

As well as getting the exposure right, you must also make sure that your subject is in focus. Most cameras now have sophisticated autofocus (AF) systems, but these can easily be fooled.

Foliage can confuse AF systems. Switch to manual focusing for best results.

123 Off-center subjects

If your subject falls outside the focus detector in the viewfinder, the camera will focus on something else, which may leave you with your principal subject out of focus.

124 Getting off-center subjects sharp

Using the viewfinder, center your subject in the AF detector. (In compact cameras, this is usually the center of the viewfinder; with some DSLRs you can select different areas of the viewfinder to be the active AF sensor.) Press the shutter release halfway to activate and lock AF. Recompose the image, then fully depress the shutter release to take the picture.

125 Fast-moving subjects

When photographing fast-moving subjects it can be better to preset the focus, wait for the subject to move into the frame of focus, and then take the picture.

126 Pre-focusing

Select a point that you know the subject will pass through. Focus on this point by depressing the shutter release halfway to lock AF and wait for the subject to enter the frame. When it reaches the point of focus, fully depress the shutter button.

Use pre-focusing techniques for fast moving subjects.

127 Obscure objects

Objects in front of, or behind, the main subject can interfere with the AF system. This is particularly so if, for example, you are looking through foliage or a fence.

128 Focusing through glass

If you are trying to focus through glass (e.g. a window or screen), reflections on the glass may confuse the AF sensor. The best option is to switch to manual focus if you have the option.

129 The plane of focus

There is only one absolute plane of focus. Anything in front of or behind that plane will be out of focus—although it may appear to be acceptably sharp if there is enough depth of field.

130 Depth of field

Depth of field is the area in front of and behind the plane of focus within which objects appear acceptably sharp. How far this area extends depends on three things:
- the lens aperture used
- the focal length of the lens
- the camera-to-subject distance.

Anything outside the range of available depth of field is blurred.

131 Lens aperture

Depth of field increases as lens aperture gets smaller (denoted by a higher f/number)—so a lens aperture of f/16 will give greater depth of field than an aperture of f/11. It will be at its minimum with the aperture wide open (smallest f/number), and at its maximum when the aperture is set to the smallest setting (highest f/number).

132 Lens focal length

The focal length of the lens will also affect the depth of field. Smaller focal length lenses, such as a wide-angle lens (e.g. 20mm), will produce more depth of field than telephoto lenses (e.g. 200mm). Therefore, depth of field will be greater on a 28mm lens set at f/8 than on a 200mm lens set at the same aperture.

133 Camera-to-subject distance

The farther from the camera the subject is, the greater the depth-of-field available. Consequently, depth of field is very limited in close-up and macro photography.

134 Using depth of field

Depth of field can be used as a compositional tool to help convey your visual ideas. For example, you can use it to create a sense of place, to isolate subjects, or to define the relationship between distant objects within a scene.

135 Acceptable depth of field

What we perceive to be acceptable sharpness varies depending on the extent of the visible blur, which, in turn, will depend on the size of the enlargement. The larger you intend to make the final print, the greater the depth of field required.

A small aperture gives increased depth of field.

136 Hyperfocal distance

The hyperfocal distance is the focus setting that gives maximum depth of field for any particular lens aperture. This is a simple and effective technique, although it can only be achieved with a lens that can be manually focused. To set the hyperfocal distance, first set the lens focus to infinity (denoted by the ∞ marking on the lens barrel). Then, using the depth of field index on the lens barrel*, note the nearest point of acceptable sharpness for the aperture you're using and adjust the focus to this distance. You have now achieved the hyperfocal distance.

* Many zoom lenses do not carry a depth of field index, in which case you'll need to use the depth of field preview button on the camera (if there is one), or refer to the depth of field tables in the lens manual.

Digital ISO

In the days of film, the "ISO" rating referred to a film's sensitivity to light—in other words, the speed at which it captured a scene. Fast films could grab images quickly and also be used in low light conditions, while slower films needed more light but produced less grainy images. Digital cameras free you from these restrictions and let you change the ISO setting for each image.

137 What is digital ISO?

In the digital era, you're no longer locked into shooting at the speed of the film in your camera. The ISO idea still remains, though strictly it is "ISO equivalency," (ISO-E) as the original ISO (International Standards Organization) scale was designed for rating film. Most cameras allow you to change the ISO of the sensor, with a growing number offering settings ranging from 100 (slow) to 1600 (faster), or even faster for some DSLRs. Each frame can be exposed at a different ISO value, so you are not limited to a single setting (or wasting a roll of film).

Image shot at 100 ISO

138 Adjusting sensitivity

Entry-level digital cameras usually have a chip sensitivity that is fixed by the manufacturer, but as you start to pay a little more, the level of control over the camera's ISO setting begins to increase. Most middle-of-the-range and "prosumer" (pro/consumer) cameras contain a variety of sensitivities. Changing the ISO is usually a matter of holding down the ISO button while turning a command dial. The changed setting is reflected in the LCD screen at the back of the camera and, in some cases, in the viewfinder as well.

Image shot at 200 ISO

139 The Auto ISO setting

Some cameras also contain an Auto ISO setting that can be selected instead of specific sensitivity values. This feature keeps the camera at the best quality option, usually 100, when the photographer is shooting under normal conditions, but will change the setting to a higher value automatically if the light starts to fade. It's a good idea to use this option as your camera's default setting. It works well in most situations and you can always change to manual when specific action or low-light scenarios arise.

Image shot at 800 ISO

140 Choosing ISO settings manually

Alternatively, you can select the sensitivity of the chip manually by choosing the ISO value to suit the lighting scenario. Use low values for scenes with plenty of light and higher settings for low-light situations.

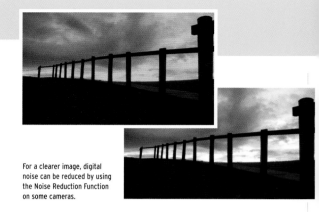

For a clearer image, digital noise can be reduced by using the Noise Reduction Function on some cameras.

141 Low ISO equals crisper pictures

If you decide to select your ISO manually, or let the camera automatically adjust the chip's sensitivity for you, always keep in mind that choosing the lowest setting possible will give you the sharpest and best-quality images overall—so use it when you can!

142 Watch out for digital noise

Although you can change the ISO setting for each and every image, you are not completely free from the issues associated with ISO ratings from the days of film. Just as fast films tend to produce grainy images, so higher digital ISO settings produce noisier images. Digital noise occurs because of the electromagnetic properties of the camera's sensor and appears as unrelated and adjacent pixels. It produces a similar appearance to the grain of photographic film, though less attractive. The bigger the enlargement of the image, the more noticeable the noise becomes.

143 Digital noise and shutter speed

At fast shutter speeds the proportion of noise relative to image pixels is very small and therefore generally can't be seen. However, the longer the sensor is active (i.e. exposed to light), the greater the ratio of noise to image pixels and the more obvious it becomes.

144 Noise reduction

Some cameras come with a "noise reduction" option specifically for use in long-time exposures. I would highly recommend using this when your shutter speeds exceed one second.

145 No sharpening when using high ISO values

When using higher ISO settings, turn off or set to minimum the camera's Sharpening feature, as this tends to exaggerate any noise present in the image. Apply sharpening afterward in your image-editing program.

146 Match sensitivity to image quality

Sensitivity in digital terms is based on how quickly your camera's sensor reacts to light. The more sensitive a sensor is, the less light is needed to capture a well-exposed image. This means that higher shutter speeds and smaller aperture numbers can be used with fast sensors (higher ISO ratings). Sports shooters in particular need cameras with sensitive chips to freeze the action, and you need a sensitive chip for photographing in low-light situations as well. But as faster/higher ISO settings produce greater noise, you will need to weigh up the merits of higher sensitivity with the disadvantages of lower image quality when choosing what ISO value to use for a specific shooting task.

White balance control

If you shoot a piece of white paper under florescent light, it will appear green; lit by an incandescent household bulb, it will look yellow. The color balance of artificial light is different from daylight, so you need to help the sensor by compensating using the camera's White Balance (WB) controls.

147 A digital solution

Film photographers were aware of the problems of shooting white objects under different light sources for years. They carried a range of color-conversion filters to help change the light source to suit the film. Digital camera producers, on the other hand, address the problem by including White Balance (WB) controls. These features adjust the captured image to suit the lighting conditions under which it is photographed. The most basic models usually provide Automatic White Balancing (AWB), but other cameras have a number of choices for correcting the problem.

General White Balance modes include:
- Auto
- Fine or Daylight
- Incandescent
- Fluorescent
- Cloudy
- Flash (Speedlight)
- Preset or Custom

Many modern digital cameras contain sophisticated White Balance options under the WB menu.

Different colored light sources are responsible for the strange casts you sometimes see in your images.

148 Auto White Balance

The Auto White Balance (AWB) function assesses the color of the light in the general environment and attempts to neutralize the midtones of the image. As with most auto camera features, this setting works well for the majority of "normal" scenarios, but you may have some difficulty with subjects that are predominantly one color, or which are lit from behind. Also keep in mind that some subjects are meant to have a slight color shift from pure white and so the use of the Auto feature in this case would remove the subtle hue of the original. If in doubt, try the Auto setting first. Check the results on the preview screen of the camera and if a color cast remains, then move onto more specific options.

The Auto setting assesses the light falling on your subject and sets the white balance options automatically.

149 Light-source white balance settings

The Daylight (Fine), Tungsten or Incandescent (for household bulbs), Fluorescent, Cloudy, and Flash (Speedlight) options are designed for each of these light types. The manufacturers have examined the color from a variety of these sources, averaged the results, and produced a setting to suit. For those times when the source you are using differs from the norm, however, some cameras have a fine-tuning adjustment. With the light source set, turn the command dial to adjust the color settings. For Daylight, Incandescent, Cloudy, and Flash options, selecting positive values increases the amount of blue in the image. Alternatively, negative numbers increase the red content. If you have selected Fluorescent as your light source, fine-tuning feature allows you to select one of three different WB settings. FL1 is suitable for tubes marked "white," FL2 should be used with "daylight white" tubes, and FL3 is for those labeled "daylight."

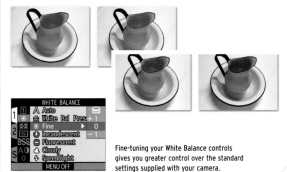

Fine-tuning your White Balance controls gives you greater control over the standard settings supplied with your camera.

Option	Bulb Type
FL1	White (W)
FL2	Daylight White (Neutral [N])
FL3	Daylight (D)

Three different fluorescent settings are provided with some cameras so you can fine-tune your WB settings for this light source.

The Auto White Balance Bracketing features available in some cameras captures several images with different settings, giving you the opportunity to select the best result back at the desktop.

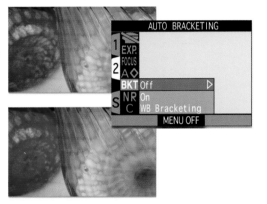

150 Applying fine-tuning automatically

If you find that manual fine-tuning hampers the flow of your photography–shoot, stop, switch to menu, fine-tune white balance, shoot again, stop, switch to menu, and so on–then check to see if your camera has an Auto White Balance Bracketing option. This feature automatically shoots a series of three images, starting with the standard white balance settings and then adding a little blue and finally a little red. White balance bracketing is particularly useful when shooting difficult subjects, such as the hand-blown colored glass shown in the example (right). As three separate images are saved, you can make decisions about the most appropriate color by previewing them on your monitor later rather than the small preview screen on the back of your camera in the field.

151 Customizing your White Balance

In reality, most scenarios are illuminated by a variety of different-colored lights. For instance, a simple portrait taken in your room might have the subject partially lit by the incandescent lamp stand in the corner, the fluorescent tube on the dining room ceiling, and the daylight coming through the windows. Here you should use the Customize White Balance option. Based on video technology, this works by measuring the light's combined color as it falls onto a piece of white paper. The camera then compares this reading with a reference white in its memory and designs a setting for your scenario. It takes into account changes in color that result from:
- light reflecting off brightly painted walls
- bulbs getting older
- mixed light sources
- light streaming through colored glass
- shooting through colored filters.

152 Calibrate your monitor!

If you are going to view the images later on your desktop monitor and check for color casts, then ensure that you regularly calibrate your monitor so that you know it is displaying colors accurately.

Shooting objects that appear white to the human eye under artificial light sources confuses cameras and creates whites that have a green or yellow "color cast." The WB function compensates for the color of the light source.

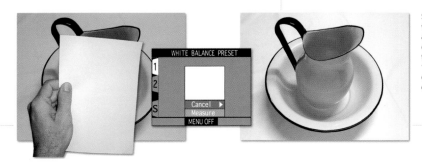

Image quality—getting the best

The manner in which digital cameras are marketed would have you think that megapixels are the only factor in image quality. Not so. File type, compression, image size, and numerous other in-camera settings will all affect the quality of the image that is finally stored on the memory card. The following advice will help you to define the level of quality you need and how to achieve it.

153 What are pixels?

A digital sensor is an array of photodiodes laid out in a grid pattern. Simply put, these create pixels (picture elements) and, in very general terms, the greater the number of pixels, the higher the image resolution.

154 What is resolution?

Resolution is the measure of the total number of pixels on the sensor (width x height). For example, an image sensor measuring 3,072 pixels across x 2,048 pixels high has a resolution of 6,291,456 pixels, more commonly referred to as 6.2 megapixels.

155 Resolution and image quality

It makes sense that a sensor with 10 million pixels or "points" for capturing light will produce a better image than a sensor with, say, half the capability. In basic terms, this is true. However, because an element of image quality is dependent on how many of those pixels are used for image capture (effective pixels), as well as a number of varying parameters, such as their size, shape, and configuration, the world of digital resolution is less simple than that.

156 Dynamic range and image quality

Photodiodes are sensitive only to a certain range of brightness levels (known as the sensor's dynamic range), and this range varies between sensors from different manufacturers. The higher the dynamic range, the greater the amount of information that can be captured. Therefore, it's feasible that a camera with a lower number of total pixels than another can sometimes have a higher resolution.

157 Pixels and picture use

What is important is the number of pixels you actually need, and that depends on what you intend to do with the photograph. For use only on a website or for small prints for a scrapbook, say, then resolution is less important. For prints and professional publication, high resolution is very important. For example, many photo agencies will only accept images with a file size of between 40MB and 50MB.

3 x 2

6 x 4

7 x 5

158 Resolution and print size

The following table provides a quick reference for resolution requirements when printing. This table is based on printing at 300 dots per inch (dpi), which is the "gold standard" for inkjet printers. You may find you're happy with results achieved with a resolution of 240dpi. To a certain degree the result will depend on the type of image, and what you consider is "good enough" when viewed from an acceptable viewing distance.

Minimum resolution for print size

Print size (in)	Minimum pixel dimensions
3 x 2	900 x 600 = 0.5 megapixels
6 x 4	1,800 x 1,200 = 2.2 megapixels
7 x 5	2,100 x 1,500 = 3.1 megapixels
10 x 8	3,000 x 2,400 = 7.2 megapixels

10 x 8

159 Total pixels and effective pixels?

Camera manufacturers usually provide two pixel counts with their marketing blurb: total pixels and effective pixels. When determining image resolution, only effective pixels are relevant, and provide a more accurate indication of image resolution. This is because some of the pixels on a sensor are used for tasks other than recording brightness levels.

160 Setting image size

In general terms, the larger the size of the image the better, remembering that it's always possible to reduce file size but never to increase it without compromising image quality. When shooting in JPEG mode, your camera will typically give three file-size options—small, medium, and large.

161 Medium and small file sizes

The advantage of selecting a size other than large is that it reduces the amount of space the image takes up on the memory card. It may also increase burst-rate. The significant disadvantage is that it greatly reduces image quality. If the images are intended for quick transmission via the Internet, and quality is of little concern, then a small image size may be acceptable.

162 Large file sizes

If you intend to print your images at anything beyond postcard size, or to use your images professionally, then you will want to select a large image size.

163 Selecting the file type

Most digital cameras can save images as either JPEG files or RAW files—the name may vary depending on the particular brand of your camera. Some cameras also have a TIFF file type as well. Which type is better for your photography depends largely on what you plan to do with the pictures afterward.

164 Resolution and image quality

It makes sense that a sensor with 10 million pixels or "points" for capturing light will produce a better image than a sensor with, say, half the capability. In basic terms, this is true. However, because an element of image quality is dependent on how many of those pixels are used for image capture (effective pixels), as well as a number of varying parameters, such as their size, shape, and configuration, the world of digital resolution is less simple than that.

165 RAW files

RAW files are saved unprocessed by the camera. The camera makes a note of the settings applied at the time the image was taken and attaches this "note" to the raw data. It then saves the image either compressed (using lossless compression technology) or uncompressed to the memory card with a unique name and RAW extension (which is specific to the manufacturer), such as NIKO010.nef (NEF is Nikon's proprietary RAW extension name).

Advantages of shooting in RAW mode

166 Unprocessed work

Having a RAW file is the equivalent of having exposed but unprocessed film. It holds only the data captured at the scene without any other variables applied, which means you can use different processing techniques as frequently as you like, taking advantage of new and improved software applications as they're developed.

167 Later adjustments

Shooting parameters such as WB, sharpening, saturation, etc., can be adjusted after the picture has been taken, as though they were set at the time of shooting, which minimizes the likelihood of image degradation. It's a little like having the ability to retrace your steps and reshoot the scene as often as you like. Arguably, these parameters can also be adjusted on a JPEG file, but alterations cannot be made with the same accuracy and exactness.

168 Color conversion

Color conversion is done in-computer (using more sophisticated algorithms than the camera's built-in processors can handle), which improves image quality.

169 16-bit mode

RAW files take advantage of the full 16-bit mode in-computer, giving a total of 65,536 brightness levels to work with, as opposed to just 256 with a JPEG file. This makes post-camera processing a far more expansive application and gives you greater image-processing options than are available with JPEGs.

170 RAW to JPEG

You can create a JPEG file from a RAW file, but you can't create a RAW file from a JPEG. Similarly, you can compress a large file to make it smaller, but once the JPEG algorithms have discarded their data, you can never be sure of recreating it exactly.

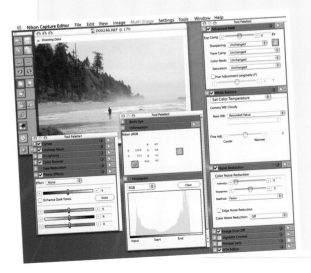

Advantages of shooting in JPEG mode

 Formats and file sizes

JPEGs produce much smaller files, hence more can be shot per memory card. For example, a 512MB card will store about 222 high-resolution, or 1300 low-resolution JPEGs, compared to just 79 RAW images. Similarly, the burst-rate is affected. You could shoot 40 consecutive high-resolution JPEGs and only 25 RAW images on the same camera—a loss of well over one-third in productivity.

172 JPEG versus RAW

While you can argue the limitations of JPEG-processing algorithms, the reality is that there is very little visible difference between a high-resolution JPEG (referred to as a FINE JPEG both in Nikon and Canon) and a RAW file for most uses.

173 Online service

Because JPEG files are smaller in size, they can be transmitted more easily over the Internet or a computer network.

174 On JPEG time

Because JPEG files are processed in-camera, you can produce finished images of high quality before downloading them to a computer, which makes post-camera processing less necessary. So, if you prefer to spend time taking pictures in the field, then JPEGs will help reduce the time you need to spend in front of a computer.

175 Image-editing software

JPEGs can be opened in practically any graphics software application, which negates the need for the proprietary software supplied by the camera's manufacturer. This can save time in the digital workflow because it removes one stage from the overall process.

176 RAW versus JPEG

Many DSLRs now have a function that enables you to capture both RAW and JPEG images simultaneously. This has the advantage that you get to have your cake and eat it, with regard to speed versus quality. However, the disadvantage is that you increase the overall file size, which reduces the effective capacity of the memory card.

177 Speed versus quality

At the end of the day, whether you shoot RAW or JPEG files comes down to the final application. If image quality is less important than speed of delivery, then shoot JPEG. If image quality is everything, then shoot RAW. If in doubt, and if your model of camera supports it, shoot in RAW+JPEG mode, and you have the best of both worlds.

 +

178 TIFF images

Some cameras support the TIFF file extension. TIFF files, like JPEGs, are processed in-camera and so have none of the advantages of RAW files. They are also very large files, so lack the size advantage of JPEGs. The one advantage they do share with the RAW image is that any compression applied is lossless. However, there are few applications that would require you to shoot TIFF in-camera.

179 Converting RAW files

Eventually, all RAW files have to be converted into a more standard file type, such as TIFF or JPEG. All RAW files have a proprietary extension (Nikon=NEF; Canon=CRW), which determines the code used when constructing a RAW file. Because this code is unique to a particular manufacturer, generally the file must be opened in that manufacturer's proprietary software. For example, Nikon RAW NEF files must be opened in Nikon View or Nikon Capture software. It's fair to say that some of these applications are less than ideal for image-processing, and sometimes vary from camera to camera, making standardization of your workflow impossible.

180 Generic RAW conversion software

There are some generic image-processing applications that include RAW file converters, or translators, that allow RAW files to be opened independently from the proprietary software. For example, Photoshop contains translators that allow RAW files to be opened directly within the application.

181 JPEG compression

When a file is compressed using JPEG compression, algorithms are used to reduce the physical size of the image file (in bytes). Once the file is compressed, some original data are discarded permanently. When the file is opened, algorithms are again used to reconstruct the image, with the missing data replaced with simulated pixels, often resulting in a loss of image quality.

182 Resaving JPEG files

Every time you resave a JPEG file it is further compressed. Eventually, if resaved over and over, there will be little left of the original data. If you plan on regularly processing the same image, then it is better to save the image as a TIFF file.

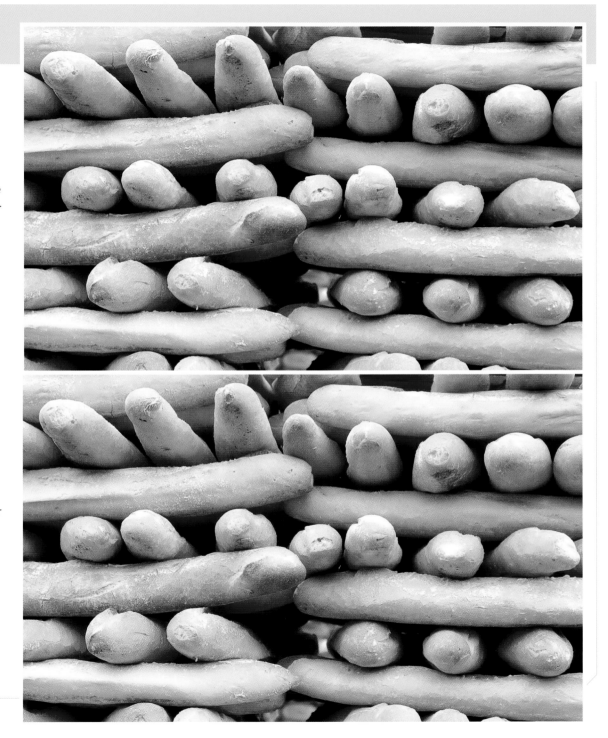

FINE = 1:16 (1 pixel in 16)

NORMAL = 1:8 (1 pixel in 8)

BASIC = 1:4 (1 pixel in 4)

183 Reducing the negative effects of JPEG compression

Typically, there are three levels of in-camera JPEG compression—FINE, NORMAL, and BASIC. The compression ratios used in each are roughly as follows:

FINE = 1:16 (1 pixel in 16)
NORMAL = 1:8 (1 pixel in 8)
BASIC = 1:4 (1 pixel in 4)

184 RAW (and TIFF) compression

Lossless compression, as applied to RAW and TIFF files, compresses the data to reduce the file size but retains all the original data. When the file is retrieved, the computer reconstructs the image with exactly the same data that it started with, and image quality is maintained at the original level, and file sizes are therefore larger.

185 Other effects of compression

In some camera models, applying file compression in-camera can significantly slow down the processing time, which in turn adversely affects the burst-rate. In others, compression actually speeds up the processing of images between the internal memory and the memory card.

Keep it steady

If you want to get the most from your cameras and lenses and produce photographs that are as sharp as a razor, you'll need to learn how to support them.

186 How to hold your camera

How you hold your camera can make all the difference between a picture being pin sharp or ruined by camera shake.

- Stand with your back straight and your feet slightly apart.
- Hold the camera with both hands and tuck your elbows into your side to aid stability.
- Squeeze the shutter and release gently rather than jabbing it.
- Depress the shutter after exhaling so your body is relaxed rather than tense.
- Kneeling or sitting down will provide more stability when using long or heavy lenses.

187 Support the camera

If light levels are low and you're forced to work at a shutter speed that's too slow for handholding, look for things that can be used to help keep the camera steady.

- Press the camera against a post or tree and use that to provide stability.
- Rest the camera on a wall or post, perhaps using a jacket or camera bag to cushion it.
- Use the frame of an open car window as a support.

188 Tripod choice

A tripod provides the best form of camera support, allowing you to use exposures of seconds, minutes, even hours, and still produce sharp images. Buy a model that will extend to eye level without the need for a center column, and make sure it's solidly built. Carbon-fiber tripods are ideal, as they're lighter than alloy models but just as stable.

189 Ultimate image quality

Achieving ultimate image quality is easy if you're willing to put a little effort into your photography.

- Keep your camera's ISO as low as possible—whether digital or film, the lower the ISO the sharper the image will be. As ISO increases, noise/grain become more obvious.
- Buy the best lenses and filters you can afford and keep them clean—dust and grime on optical surfaces reduces image quality.
- Lenses generally give their best optical performance in the middle of the aperture range (f/8–f/11) and their worst at the widest and narrowest aperture settings.
- Mount your camera on a sturdy tripod and trip the shutter with a cable release to avoid camera shake.

Composition

The rule of thirds

Balance is often the key to compositional success, and one technique that will help you achieve that is the good old rule of thirds.

190 Creating the grid

To use the rule of thirds you need to divide your camera's viewfinder into an imaginary grid of nine segments, using two vertical and two horizontal lines—as shown above right. Focusing screens marked with a grid are useful here, but it's possible to imagine the grid quite easily.

191 Positioning the focal point

To achieve compositional balance when using the rule of thirds, place your main focal point on one of the four intersection points created by the imaginary lines. The focal point is the element in a composition that you want the viewer to be drawn to—whatever it may be.

192 Vertical features

Use the two vertical lines in the grid to help you position strong vertical elements and divide the frame in a more visually interesting way—a person can be placed off-center, for example, as can other features such as trees and buildings.

195 Make the most of foreground interest

When shooting landscapes, you will normally want to emphasize the foreground. To do this, place the horizon on the higher horizontal line of your imaginary grid, so the sky only occupies the top third of the picture area and the foreground fills the rest.

193 More than one focal point

A composition can have more than one focal point, but to avoid a cluttered composition, care is required when it comes to their placement in the frame. Use the rule of thirds if you can, at least for the primary focal point, and shoot from an angle that allows the eye to move from one focal point to the next.

194 Emphasize the sky

If you want to make the most of a dramatic sky, position the horizon on the lower horizontal line in the grid so the landscape occupies the bottom third of the frame and the sky occupies the rest.

196 Don't force it

Although the rule of thirds is a handy compositional aid, don't force your pictures to conform to it—not every scene or subject will suit this treatment. Anyway, aren't rules there to be broken?

Composing with Color

Colors can be warm or cold, strong or weak. They can harmonize or contrast and vary in tone from bold primaries to subtle secondaries. One thing's for certain though: color, and the way you use it, can make or break a photograph because it has a huge impact on the reaction of the viewer.

197 The color wheel

Light is formed by the colors of the spectrum, which we also see when a rainbow is formed. Arranging these colors around a wheel is a good way of understanding how they relate to one another. On one side, there are the warm colors—magenta, red, and yellow—and on the other, the colder—green, cyan, and blue. These are the primary colors (red, green, and blue) and their complementaries (cyan, magenta, and yellow). Colors on opposite sides of the color wheel are said to clash or contrast, while colors that are close together harmonize.

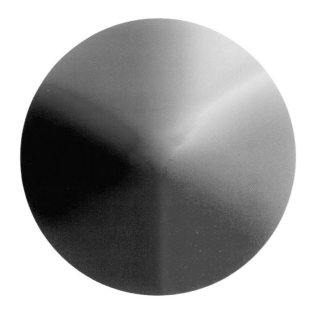

198 Quality of light

The way colors record outdoors is influenced by the quality of light. Early and late in the day the light is naturally very warm, so colors appear warm. In the middle of the day, with the sun overhead, the light has a slight coolness, so colors appear cooler. Color saturation is at its highest when the light is slightly diffused rather than the hard light of full sun. Colors appear very rich in open shade because the light is soft and contrast low. Backlighting reduces color saturation.

199 Weather conditions

The weather affects the quality of light in a big way. In clear, sunny weather, colors appear bright and well saturated. Different colors are also clearly defined. Dull, overcast weather makes colors appear much softer, while mist merges colors, making the difference between warm and cold hues less obvious and all colors to appear to harmonize because they are so muted. Dense fog can make a normally colorful scene appear monochromatic.

200 Contrasting colors

Colors opposite each other on the color wheel are said to contrast—such as yellow and blue or red and green. Including them together in a picture works well because the resulting image jars the senses and attracts attention. For the best results, shoot in strong light and include the colors in equal quantity so that one doesn't dominate the other.

201 Harmonious colors

Colors that are close to each other on the color wheel harmonize–such as yellow and red, yellow and green, green and blue, and so on. Different shades of the same color also harmonize well. Color harmony is useful in composition because it allows you to produce images that are easy on the eye. Think of the warm colors of a woodland scene in fall or the glow of sunrise or sunset.

Color temperature

As a means of measuring the color differences in light–rather than just saying it's a bit blue or a bit orange–photographers use a system known as the Kelvin scale (K), which refers to light in terms of its color temperature. Normal light–the type you find on a clear, sunny afternoon–has a color temperature around 5,500 K, and colors record naturally. If color temperature rises above 5,500 K the light becomes cooler, and colors take on a slight blue cast, as on a dull day; if color temperature drops below 5,500 K it becomes warmer, and colors take on a yellow/orange cast, as at sunrise and sunset.

Our eyes adapt to these changes in the color temperature of light, so colors always appear more or less natural. However, photographic film and digital sensors can't–they record light as it really is–so steps may need to be taken to avoid unwanted color casts. With film you can use colored filters (as recommended below). With digital cameras you can use Auto White Balance (AWB) or change the Kelvin sensitivity of your camera's sensor using the White Balance setting.

Color casts aren't always undesirable, of course. The color temperature at sunset can be as low as 3,000 K, but you wouldn't want to filter out the warmth in the light because it makes your pictures look far more attractive.

Light source	Color temp	Filtration
Shade under blue sky	7500K	Orange 85B
Under cloudy sky	7000K	81D warm
Average daylight	5500K	None
Electronic flash	5500K	None
Afternoon sunlight	4500K	NR
Early morning/evening sunlight	3500K	NR
Tungsten photofloods	3400K	Blue 80B
Sunrise/sunset	3000K	NR
Domestic tungsten bulbs	2800k	Blue 80A + 80C

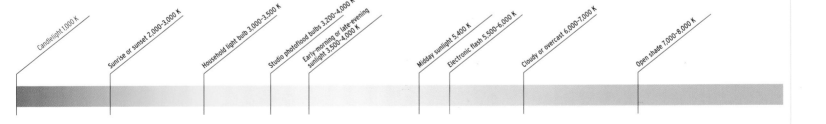

202 Single color

You can produce stunning pictures of scenes comprising just one color or the same color in different shades. Soft, hazy backlighting tends to create this effect in nature by bringing the colors closer together, but you'll also find manmade evidence of it too in the use of building materials and paint color.

203 Increasing color saturation

Slight underexposure of a photograph will make colors more deeply saturated. This works with both film and digital cameras, but you need to be careful not to overdo it, otherwise colors appear dark and muddy.

204 Warm colors

Warm colors—such as orange and yellow—help to create images with a tranquil, soothing effect, especially when the tones are soft and gentle. This is why landscape photographers prefer to shoot at dawn and dusk, when daylight is naturally warm.

205 Monochromatic color

When a scene or subject consists of a single color or different shades of the same color, then that color is said to be monochromatic. Haze and dust can create this effect, especially at sunrise and sunset, when you shoot into the light and everything takes on a beautiful golden glow. The effect of this limited color palette can produce photographs full of atmosphere.

206 Cold colors

In cold or dull weather color bias moves toward blue, and the feel of your photographs will change completely, having a more somber, melancholy feel that can be just as effective as warm colors.

207 Graduated filters

Add color to insipid skies using colored graduated filters. Pink, mauve, pale red, and orange can add impact to photographs taken at sunrise and sunset—but don't expect the results to look natural.

209 Colors that advance

Colors at the warm end of the spectrum are said to advance, because they stand out and demand attention. Red is the most powerful color in this respect, which is why it can dominate a photograph even when it only occupies a small area. Yellows and oranges also do this.

208 Abstract color

You can produce striking abstract images by exploiting areas of bold color and composing a subject or scene so that the colors are emphasized rather than the forms. Try excluding part of your subject so the obvious center of attention is missing, or frame it from an unusual angle.

210 Colors that recede

Cool colors—blues and greens—are said to recede. This makes them great as background colors as they help to make other colors stand out, which is why areas of blue sky are so effective in photographs.

211 Dominant colors

Don't always be tempted to fill the frame with bold, clashing colors—a photograph will often be more successful if you let one powerful hue dominate the image so it becomes the focus of attention. The more intense the color, the more it will dominate, especially if it appears in the background to a more neutral or softer color.

212 Color symbolism

The primary colors have great symbolic value, which you can use to great effect in your photographs:

- Red reminds us of anger, danger, love, passion, blood, and fire.
- Blue can be both soothing—it's symbolic of the sky, water, purity, and wide-open spaces—but, equally, it can be a cold, depressing color that reminds us of bad weather, loneliness, and sadness.
- Green is the color of nature—trees, fields, and hills. It symbolizes the great outdoors, new life, freshness, and vibrancy.
- Yellow is light, the sun, and pure gold. It's a happy, positive color that makes photographs soothing to look at and easy on the eye.

213 Isolating color

Use your telezoom or telephoto lens to isolate interesting areas of color and to exclude unwanted details from the frame. Changing camera angle may also allow you to create more interesting juxtapositions of colors.

214 Using color filters

Add color to your photographs with filters. The pale amber 81-series of warm-up filters are ideal for enhancing pictures taken at sunrise and sunset, while the pale blue 82-series filters will enhance cool colors and are ideal for shooting in dull, misty, or foggy weather. For a stronger color cast, use the blue 80-series and orange 85-series of color-conversion filters.

215 Make the most of your polarizer

A polarizing filter removes glare from nonmetallic surfaces and cuts through haze to make colors appear more deeply saturated, so use it whenever you want your photographs to have maximum impact. Don't limit its use to bright sunlight either—in dull, damp weather, glare is increased, so your polarizer will still do a great job of boosting colors. To deepen blue sky, keep the sun at roughly 90 degrees to the camera.

216 Increase the atmosphere

When the light is soft and hazy and colors are muted you can create beautiful, atmospheric images. To enhance the mood, use a soft-focus filter or breathe on the lens to create a misty effect. This works particularly well when you're shooting into the light and the subject is backlit.

217 Something from nothing

Why not set yourself a project to shoot a series of pictures where color is the sole subject? For example, your theme could be a given color, and your challenge is to find interesting things of that color to photograph. It's a great way to develop your eye for a picture.

218 Go close for impact

One of the most common compositional mistakes is not getting close enough to the main subject. So from now on, no matter how close you are, always take a few steps toward your subject and see what a difference it makes. Fill the frame with color.

219 Red-enhancing filter

This filter deepens colors at the warm end of the spectrum, especially reds, and it is ideal for photographs where warm hues dominate, such as the color of trees in the fall or landscapes at sunrise and sunset. A special glass called didymium is used in the filter's construction to achieve this effect.

221 Hand-coloring

A color photograph doesn't have to start out in color—why not make a black-and-white version of your image by selectively desaturating it using image-editing software so only parts of it remain in color, or desaturating the whole image then adding color back so it looks like a hand-colored photograph.

220 Make your own pictures

You can create striking color photographs by collecting together interesting objects and composing still lifes. Place vibrant yellow flowers against a blue background, for example, and you have a powerful color contrast; children's toys and colorful items such as plastic picnic sets also make great subjects for color close-ups.

222 Twilight zone

Before the sun has risen or after it has set, the landscape is lit by light reflected from the sky so it often takes on a surreal blue cast that looks incredibly atmospheric. This is best seen in coastal areas as the color of the sky is reflected in the sea. Use long exposures to blur motion in the sea and add mood.

223 Sunrise and sunset

The light is at its most magical at dawn and dusk. Before sunrise and after sunset clouds are often uplit by the sun, which is below the horizon, so the sky is full of beautiful colors. When the sun is close to the horizon, golden light rakes across the landscape and casts long, cool shadows that reveal texture and form.

225 Manmade color

Various forms of artificial illumination—including sodium vapor, fluorescent, mercury vapor, and tungsten—create vivid color casts that can produce surprising effects when photographed because our eyes adapt to the casts so we don't realize they are there. These are best recorded in towns and cities at night, when the average street scene will contain an amazing mixture of light sources, each creating their own colors.

224 Making bluebells blue

It is notoriously difficult to photograph bluebells and make their color reproduce accurately. One solution is to use an inverted pale blue graduated filter to cover the bottom part of the picture area where the flowers are. Results are also better in overcast weather when the light is soft. Finally, careful adjustments in Photoshop using Color Balance or the Hue/Saturation slider may help.

226 Correcting color casts

You can use filters and Photoshop controls to get rid of unusual color casts, but don't be too eager to do so—often their strange and vibrant colors can improve a photograph, as you'll discover when shooting the urban landscape at night.

227 Adjusting white balance

Instead of always shooting with your digital camera set to AWB, experiment with different settings. Set Tungsten when shooting in daylight and your pictures will record with a cold, blue cast. Set to Cloudy and your pictures will appear warmer—great at sunrise and sunset.

Perspective and scale

Photography may be a two-dimensional medium, but if you want to produce pictures with impact, you need to find ways of adding depth.

228 What is perspective?

Perspective is the impression of depth that is created by the spatial relationship between the elements in a scene. Our brain looks for clues to establish which elements are close and which are farther away. By using the same clues when composing a photograph you can create the illusion of three dimensions, even though the photograph only has two.

229 Lenses and perspective

Although perspective doesn't actually change, the type of lens (or focal-length setting) you use will give the impression that it does. Wide-angle lenses make the elements in a scene seem more widely spaced, while telephoto lenses appear to crowd them together. However, in reality perspective remains the same. To prove this, take one photograph with your zoom lens set to, say, 28mm, then a second of the same scene from exactly the same position with the zoom set to 200mm. If you crop a section of the wide-angle view so it shows the same area as that captured in the telephoto view and compare the two, you will see that perspective in both images is identical. Perspective only changes if you also change camera position.

230 Aerial perspective

Haze, mist, and fog may at first seem to reduce any sense of depth, but if you look carefully you will see that the layers in a scene become lighter in color or tone as distance increases. This is known as aerial perspective, and it's best captured using a telephoto or telezoom lens to fill the frame with a more distant part of the scene where the effect is stronger.

231 Linear perspective

If you include parallel lines in a photograph—such as the edges of a long, straight road, or rows of crops in a field—you will see that those lines appear to move closer together with distance. This is linear perspective. In reality the lines remain the same distance apart no matter how far away they are, but because they appear to be closer together, our brain tells us they must be moving away from the camera so distance and depth is implied. A wide-angle lens is the best tool for revealing this, and ideally you should include the vanishing point—the imaginary point in the distance where the lines appear to meet.

232 Diminishing perspective

If you photograph an avenue of trees, all roughly the same height, the tree closest to the camera will appear slightly bigger than the one next to it, and so on until the last tree appears to be a fraction the size of the first. This is diminishing perspective, or diminishing scale. Our brain tells us that the trees are all a similar size, so if one appears smaller than another it must be farther away from the camera, and a sense of depth is achieved.

233 Stretching perspective

Wide-angle lenses appear to stretch perspective by making the elements in a scene seem more widely spaced, and in doing so they create a strong sense of diminishing scale. If you move in close to a haystack in the foreground of a scene, for example, it will appear much bigger than the farmhouse in the distance—which means the house must be much farther away. This is one of the most effective ways of creating a sense of depth in a photograph.

234 Size recognition

A simple way of implying scale in a photograph is by including something of consistent and recognizable size, so the viewer can make a comparison between it and other elements that appear in the same scene. For example, if a person appears dwarfed by a waterfall, we know the waterfall must be huge.

235 Unreal scale

Scale doesn't always have to be accurate or realistic, and by intentionally breaking the rules you can create images that jolt the senses and force the viewer to take a second look. A classic example of this is the thousands of pictures taken each year of tourists appearing to hold up the Leaning Tower of Pisa with one hand—a trick created by a clever use of camera angle that makes the impossible seem possible.

236 Compressing perspective

If you photograph a scene using a telephoto lens, the elements you include will appear to be crowded together, and this can produce very simple, powerful images—think of a distant mountain range or the congested buildings in a busy city. The greater the focal length, the more pronounced this effect.

237 Creating scale

If no sense of scale appears in a scene, create your own by including a recognizable feature, such as a person or vehicle.

238 Look for patterns

Repetition makes for interesting pictures, so keep an eye out for patterns—natural or manmade—and crop out unwanted information to keep the composition simple and striking.

239 Flat light

In dull, overcast weather the light is very low in contrast so there are no discernible shadows and the world looks rather flat and two-dimensional. However, this can produce very atmospheric images—especially in black and white.

241 Eliminating scale

Excluding all clues about size and scale can produce successful photographs because they captivate the viewer and force them to try to work out just what it is they're looking at—which means their attention and interest is held.

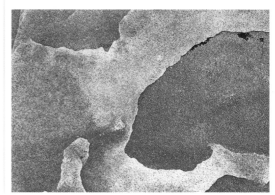

240 Side lighting

Side lighting is very effective in revealing depth because the shadows are clearly visible, and they help to accentuate texture and modeling. Think of a landscape photographed in early-morning light with the sun at 90 degrees to the camera or a portrait where your subject is lit from one side—the play of light and shade is highly effective in implying depth.

243 Put yourself in the picture

If you can't find anything to suggest scale in a scene, use yourself—compose the shot, set the self-timer, then dash into the foreground. Wearing a red jacket or holding a red umbrella will ensure you stand out and also create a strong focal point.

244 Shooting silhouettes

Despite being clearly two dimensional, silhouettes can create great images because they're so simple and striking. The main factor you have to bear in mind is that the subject you shoot forms an easily recognizable shape, otherwise you'll end up with a confusing muddle of overlapping black shapes.

245 Go for balance

A balanced composition is easier to look at and enjoy, so when using perspective and scale to give your pictures depth, remember also to work carefully with the elements in front of you, so the final photograph is ordered and harmonious.

242 Foreground interest

Including bold foreground interest in a composition is a great way to capture a strong sense of depth and scale, so always be on the lookout for suitable features when shooting landscapes.

Lines and shapes

Whether they're natural or manmade, assumed or real, lines and shapes are powerful compositional aids that can make a good picture great.

246 Leading the eye

Your aim when composing a photograph is to lead the viewer's eye into the picture and to take it on a compelling journey around the scene you're depicting. Lines in their many forms can be used to do this, and they often add a sense of depth and scale at the same time.

247 Horizontal lines

Horizontal lines echo the horizon, so are naturally passive and suggest repose. Manmade boundaries in the landscape–such as walls and fences–are obvious examples of horizontal lines that help to divide the image up into definite areas. The eye begins at the bottom of a picture and works up, so horizontal lines divide it into sections that can be observed one at a time.

248 Vertical lines

Vertical lines are more active, and they create tension in a composition–think of the lines created by electricity pylons or the soaring walls of skyscrapers. To maximize the effect, turn your camera on its side so the eye has further to travel from the bottom of the frame to the top.

249 Converging lines

Converging lines are the most powerful of all because they add a strong sense of depth to a photograph and carry the eye through the composition from foreground to background. The converging effect is best emphasized using a wide-angle lens–28mm, 24mm, or 20mm–so the lines appear wide apart in the foreground then move closer together with distance until they meet at the vanishing point.

250 Diagonal lines

Diagonal lines contrast strongly with the horizontal and vertical lines that form the borders of an image, so can create tense, dynamic compositions. As the eye tends to travel naturally from bottom left to top right, diagonal lines traveling in this direction also carry the eye through a scene from the foreground to the background.

251 Using shadows

Shadows of trees, people, buildings, telegraph poles, fences, and many other features can be used as lines in a composition. For the best results, shoot when the sun is low in the sky—early or late in the day—so shadows are long, and adjust the camera position so the shadows form horizontal, diagonal, or vertical lead-in lines. Shadows also form interesting shapes in their own right and can help you to create striking images from literally nothing.

252 Manmade

There are many examples of manmade lines—walls, fences, hedgerows, avenues of trees, furrows and planted crops, pathways, and roads, to name just a few.

253 Natural lines

Rivers and streams are the most common natural lines in the landscape. Use them to lead the eye and draw the viewer into the picture.

254 Treemendous

Fill the frame with the regimented trunks of trees to create simple, dynamic compositions. Turn the camera on its side to make the most of the vertical lines created by the trunks and use a telephoto lens to compress perspective.

255 Look for spirals

Look for subjects where the focal point is central, but the eye is then encouraged to spiral out to the edges—such as close-ups of flowers. You can also create this effect by zooming your lens during exposure.

256 "S" shapes

The curving "S" created by a meandering river or stream, or even a manmade feature such as a road, forms a perfect lead-in line, but is much more soothing and gentle than a straight line.

257 Triangles add strength

The triangle is the strongest shape, so if you can arrange the elements in a scene to form one, this will add strength to the composition. For example, three people arranged in a portrait so their heads form a triangle will produce a stronger composition than if you simply line them up. Make sure the triangle has the point at the top, otherwise imbalance will result.

258 Repeat after me

Patterns hold the attention because the repetition of features encourages the eye to look around the frame, moving from one to the next.

259 Assumed lines

Lines can be assumed as well as real. If you photograph a person looking into a scene, for example, an assumed line will be created by the direction of their gaze, simply because we can't help but follow it to see what they're looking at.

260 Symmetry and asymmetry

Photographs that are composed symmetrically appear balanced and stable and are restful to look at. However, if you want to create tension and make your pictures dynamic, go for an asymmetrical composition instead.

261 Abstract eye

A composition doesn't have to be realistic or make sense to be successful, so experiment with using shapes, lines, and colors in a more abstract way, and try to exclude all references to perspective, scale, or reality.

262 Camera angle

You can change the way lines work in a picture by adjusting the camera angle. Tilt the camera left or right, for example, and horizontal or vertical lines become diagonals that are more dynamic. Try this when shooting modern architecture.

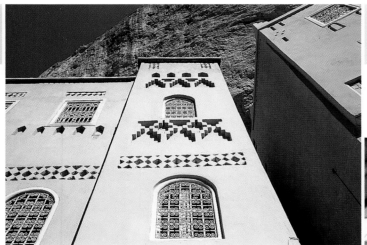

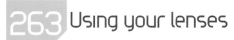

263 Using your lenses

The inherent characteristics of wide-angle and telephoto lenses will help you to make the most of lines and shapes in a scene.

264 Designing the image

In still-life photography you have the benefit of being able to decide exactly what appears in the composition, so you can start with a blank canvas and design your own pictures.

265 Develop your eye

The best way to improve your eye for a picture is simply by taking pictures, as many as you can, at every opportunity. Learn to overcome familiarity and see pictures in all situations.

266 Juxtaposing shapes

Use lens choice and viewpoint to change the relationship between the elements in a scene. Wide-angle lenses are especially useful because only a slight change of position can transform the composition due to the way they stretch perspective. The urban landscape is a great place to use this trick, as bold shapes and strong colors abound.

Framing your subject

Whether they're natural or manmade, frames can be used to enhance a composition and direct the viewer's eye toward your main subject.

267 Why framing works

Framing a scene works in the same way as framing a photograph–it adds a sympathetic border and draws attention toward the central area where the main interest is. Frames can also be used to hide distracting details and simplify compositions.

268 Doorways and windows

These both make great frames–either of the view from inside out, or from one room to the next when shooting interiors.

269 Overhanging trees

The most popular natural frame is created by the overhanging branches of trees–you can use them to frame the top of the picture like a canopy and direct the eye to the scene beyond. Branches will also help to cover up large areas of empty sky, and in doing so make the composition more interesting. Other natural frames are often found in woodland and hedgerows–just look for a gap that you can see through, then vary your distance from it to control the effective size of that gap and how much of the picture area is occupied by the frame.

270 Creating frames

If you move close enough to an object or element—the corner of a building, a wall, or a tree, for example—you can use it to help frame the scene beyond. It may not be a frame in the classic sense, but its effect on the composition will be the same.

271 Sharp or blurred?

If your frame is sharply focused it will become an integral part of the composition and demand attention. However, if you intentionally throw it out of focus by shooting at a wide aperture, the eye will tend naturally to look beyond it, so the scene you're framing will be more prominent.

272 Frames in silhouette

Frames are at their simplest and most effective when reduced to a silhouette. This is easy to achieve when the feature you are using as a frame is in shadow—such as an archway or tunnel—because, if you expose for the scene beyond it, the frame itself will be underexposed and come out black. However, you need to take care when shooting through frames that are dark and shady because they can fool your camera's metering system into overexposing the brighter scene beyond the frame. Avoid this by metering for the brighter part of the scene or walking beyond the frame to take a meter reading.

273 Simplicity counts

As with all aspects of composition, simplicity is the key. If you use a natural or manmade frame, make sure it isn't fussy or complicated, otherwise it will take attention away from your main subject and defeat the object!

Viewpoint

There's more to taking great pictures than just finding the nearest viewpoint, raising the camera to your eye, and firing away.

274 Do your homework

It pays to do a little research before visiting a new location so you have a basic idea of what to expect when you get there and can start planning your photography well in advance.

275 Shooting from eye level

Don't always take pictures with your camera held at eye level. It may be the most natural place to shoot from, but it's also the most predictable—so, if you want to capture the world in a more dynamic way, you need to get down low or climb up high.

276 Filling the frame

One of the biggest compositional mistakes photographers make is not filling the frame, so get into the habit of asking yourself, "Is this composition tight enough?" If the answer is "No," take a few steps forward or change lenses. The closer you are to your subject, the more powerful the composition is likely to be because it excludes unwanted information and concentrates the viewer's attention. Go close to increase impact.

278 Make the most of your tripod

A tripod will allow you to set up your camera in unusual spots and keep it rock solid, so you won't need to worry about camera shake when using slow shutter speeds. Make the most of this facility and capture the world from alternative angles.

279 Unusual angles

Experiment with unusual angles to give everyday subjects an interesting twist. Try tilting your camera over so that vertical lines lean—something wedding and fashion photographers often do to add impact to their pictures—although it works well with any subject because it forces the viewer to take a second look. You don't need to make excessive changes to camera position in order to transform a picture; even something as simple as kneeling down can make a big difference, as it lowers the camera and allows you to capture the world from a slightly different angle.

280 Find a high viewpoint

Shooting from the top of a tall building, bridge, or any large structure can produce stunning images—especially in busy cities where the buildings are congested and there's lots of activity at street level. Use a wide-angle lens to capture a broader view and give the impression that you were further off the ground than you really were.

277 Low viewpoints

A worm's-eye view of the world is always captivating because we're not used to seeing things from such a low vantage point. Try placing your camera on the ground and pointing up—this works great when shooting everything from people to flowers.

281 The earth from the air

For the ultimate in high viewpoints, nothing beats taking to the skies in an aircraft or hot-air balloon so you can capture the landscape stretching out below.

282 Shoot from ground level

If you don't mind getting grubby, try stretching out on your belly and shooting from ground level. You might receive a few strange looks in towns and cities, but the pictures will be great. If you're feeling really brave, try taking pictures without even looking through the camera's viewfinder—hold the camera above your head or close to the ground and fire away. You'll be surprised by the results.

283 Check maps

Detailed maps can provide lots of useful information about a location and help you to identify possible viewpoints before you leave home—as well as other features, both natural and manmade, including rivers, high ground, buildings, and roads.

284 Explore your subject

When you arrive at a location, be prepared to spend some time exploring it. By all means take the shots that immediately spring to mind but when you've done that, go for a wander to see if you can find a better viewpoint. More often than not you will, and you'll produce pictures that are a break from the norm.

285 Gaining height

If you need to shoot from a higher viewpoint, look for natural features that will increase your elevation—walls, trees, and balconies are ideal. The roof of your car can also be used—but take care not to damage it! Some landscape and architectural photographers carry stepladders in the trunks of their cars to raise camera position. This can make a big difference to the perspective you gain.

286 Try something different

If you want to produce original work, you'll need to think about ways of doing things differently from everyone else. This is especially true now the digital revolution is here, because it's easy to produce well-exposed and pin-sharp pictures—what sets a picture apart is the photographer and their imagination.

287 Get off the beaten track

If a well-worn track leads to a great view, that's because everyone goes there. However, there could be an even better view just a little way away, so always be prepared to deviate and find your own viewpoint. "The harder you work, the luckier you get." This motto applies to everything, including photography—if you're a lazy shooter your pictures will never be more than average, but if you're willing to walk the extra mile, stay out a little longer, and make the effort to explore a location fully, you'll be rewarded with great shots.

288 Look up, look down

Photographers have a tendency to look at everything from eye level, but in the urban landscape the world above your head can be just as interesting, while out in the wild you will often find fascinating details literally at your feet.

289 Check the corners

Before tripping your camera's shutter to take a picture, always spend a few seconds checking the four corners of the viewfinder to make sure unwanted or distracting elements aren't creeping in. Any that do can always be cropped out later, but composing with the intention of printing an image full frame is a good discipline to adopt.

290 Shooting through glass

Shooting through windows can give you an unusual view of the world. Colored glass will tint the scene you see through it, while old windows tend to add distortion that can work well. Remember that windows also make great frames around the view.

Break the rules

Producing original images

"To consult the rules of composition before taking a photograph is like consulting the laws of gravity before going for a walk." So said the late, great photographer Edward Weston–and he was right!

291 Rules are made to be broken

Learn the rules of composition, practice, and perfect them–but never be afraid to break them. You shouldn't compose every photograph you take to a formula, and if you were to try to, your work would quickly become predictable.

292 Horizon across the center

Start by putting the horizon across the center of the picture. Doing so produces images that are balanced and soothing to look at–perfect for tranquil landscapes, especially when you're capturing a reflection in calm water.

293 Put your main subject in the middle

If you want to create dynamic images, this is the last thing you'll want to do–but sometimes images that speak in a whisper are preferable to those that scream for attention.

294 Close to the edge

Create tension and discord by placing your main subject right at the edge of the picture. It's not what the viewer expects, so it grabs their attention–especially when the rest of the frame is empty space.

295 Jar the senses

Use clashing colors and unusual camera angles to create compositions that jar the senses. Start out composing conventionally, then do everything you can to change that.

296 Creating tension

When we look at a photograph, our reaction to it is based on a lifetime's experiences and memories that shape our visual awareness and emotional state. However, if you present an image in such a way that the viewer has nothing to compare it with, tension is created because they're not quite sure what's being said or how they should react.

297 Wide angles for portraiture

Wide-angle lenses stretch perspective. Use one really close to shoot portraits and the results will be anything but flattering because your subject's facial features will be distorted—we're talking a long nose, bulging eyes, and a big mouth!

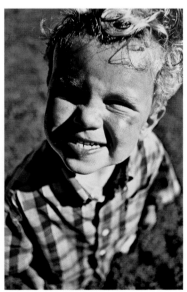

298 Shoot from unusual angles

We're used to seeing the world from a height of between 5 and 6ft (1.5-2m) off the ground, and that tends to be where most of our photographs are taken from—eye level. However, by intentionally avoiding this viewpoint and capturing familiar subjects from unusual angles, more interesting pictures will result.

299 Cut off part of your subject

If you want to create images full of intrigue, try cutting off an important part of your subject. When shooting portraits, for example, only include half the person's face—or even cut off their head altogether, so the viewer is left to wonder what they look like.

300 Obscure subjects

One way to take the viewer by surprise is by photographing things that would normally be ignored—graffiti, telephone kiosks, shop signs, trash, broken benches, etc. The more obscure the better!

301 What is it?

Try taking pictures in such a way that the viewer doesn't really know what they're looking at. Move in close, shoot with the subject out of focus, or add blur by moving the camera during exposure. Exercise your creativity: get into the habit of carrying a compact camera everywhere so you can grab pictures whenever and wherever of anything that catches your eye.

302 Let technique take over

If all you can see in a photograph is technique then it is often said to be a failure. But don't let that stop you experimenting. Use the Hue/Saturation function in Photoshop to transform an image; create infrared effects; convert parts of the image to black and white but leave the rest in color—let your imagination run riot!

303 Taking risks

The most exciting and successful photographers are the ones who take risks and try something different. Are you a risk taker?

304 Just add words

It's often said that a great photograph needs no words to describe it. Nevertheless, adding words can take your work to another creative level and allow you to influence the viewer's response to it. So why not come up with unusual titles or add lines of poetry to images?

305 Find your creative voice

It's easy to follow fashions and styles in photography, but in this digital age you need to work doubly hard if your images are to be a break from the norm. Forget about perfection and convention and do your own thing: toy cameras, pinhole, Polaroid—there are endless options.

306 Why black and white?

Because it's moody, evocative, dramatic, nostalgic, atmospheric, artistic, simple, and stunning. We may live in a colorful world, but black and white strips our world down to its bare essentials of tone, texture, shape, and form.

307 Learning to see in black and white

The key to successful black-and-white photography is in visualizing how a scene will record when stripped of its color. Try to look beyond the color itself and focus on texture, form, shape, and tone. These will become the key elements that make or break the final image.

308 How colors translate

It's important to understand how colors translate to gray tones as this can influence the tonal relationships in the final photograph. Red and green record as a similar gray tone, for example, so if red and green are the dominant colors in a scene, the final black-and-white image will look rather flat.

309 Exposing for black and white

Expose for the shadows and let the highlights take care of themselves—the opposite of how you expose for color-slide (transparency) film. This is because you need to ensure that shadow detail records on the negative.

310 Are graduated filters necessary?

Although it's common to "burn-in" or darken the sky when preparing black-and-white photographs for print, you can still use a neutral-density (ND) graduated filter when taking the photograph to lower the contrast between the sky and land. This will make it easier to print the sky because less burning-in will be required. Use a 0.6 or 0.9ND grad.

311 Using colored filters

Color filters can be used to alter the contrast and tonal balance of a black-and-white photograph. Red, orange, green, and yellow are the most popular colors. In each case, the filter lightens its own color and darkens its complimentary color.

Filter color	Effect
Yellow	Slightly darkens blue sky so white clouds stand out. Lightens skin tones and helps to hide skin blemishes. Ideal for general use, although the effect is quite subtle.
Orange	Noticeable darkening of blue and stormy skies, so adds drama. Also helps to reduce haze, hide freckles in portraits, and increases contrast. Good choice for landscape photography.
Green	Good separation of green tones makes this filter ideal for landscape and garden photography or shots of trees. It also darkens red.
Red	Blue sky goes almost black, clouds stand out starkly, and a dramatic increase in contrast allows you to create powerful pictures. Darkens greens considerably.

312 Darken the corners

A good way to frame your main subject and direct the viewer's eye toward it is by artificially darkening the corners of the print to create a gentle vignette. Do this by burning-in each corner of the image for a few seconds either when printing them in a darkroom or on image-editing software.

313 Go for grain

Photographers seem to have an obsession these days with producing pictures that are razor sharp and grain free, but in a black-and-white image coarse grain can add texture and drama to a print, so don't be afraid to use fast films, uprate, and push-process films to increase the grain—or add grain to digital images in Photoshop.

How to photograph...

Landscapes

The landscape is perhaps the most popular and accessible photographic subject—but despite that (or perhaps because the genre is so popular) it's not an easy option.

Telling a story

When you compose a landscape picture, think of it as a visual story that has a beginning to draw the viewer in, a middle that holds their attention, and an end to bring the story to a satisfying conclusion.

Depth of field

Landscapes should, in general, be sharp from the closest point to infinity. Set a small lens aperture, such as f/16 or f/22, to ensure good depth of field and use the camera's depth of field preview button (if it has one), to check whether all areas of the picture space are sharp. Many DSLR cameras have a depth of field preview button that enables you to assess depth of field accurately before the image is taken. Use it when taking landscape images to check that foreground and background detail is sharp.

316 Right place, right time

Being in the right place at the right time is a crucial factor in capturing the landscape at its best, so be prepared to work hard, accept failure, and keep going back until you get the picture you want.

317 The early bird

Oh, and be prepared to set your alarm nice and early. The best shots are often taken in the period from 30 minutes before sunrise to an hour after, because that's when the light is at its most magical and the landscape is full of atmosphere.

318 Skies

Avoid uninteresting skies, and try to include, for example, white puffy clouds against a blue sky. If the scene is worth photographing, even with a dull sky, minimize the amount of picture space the sky takes up by lowering the angle of the camera to include more foreground.

Avoid plain skies that hold no interest.

319 Fill the foreground

Strong landscapes almost always have a strong foreground to draw the viewer in and give the composition a sense of perspective and scale—so always look out for foreground interest when exploring a location.

320 Vertical versus horizontal format

Holding the camera in the vertical or horizontal format alters the emphasis on the subject in the frame. A vertical composition emphasizes height and is ideal for pictures of tall structures, such as trees and skyscrapers. A horizontal composition emphasizes space and is used widely in landscape photography.

321 The intimate landscape

Landscape photographs don't always have to be of sweeping views—small details such as ripples on a sandy beach or the colors and textures in rocks can be just as interesting.

322 The rule of thirds

The rule of thirds is a useful technique to use in landscape photography. Divide the picture frame into equal thirds both vertically and horizontally. For a compositionally strong and dynamic image, position the subject where the dividing lines intersect.

323 Black and white weather

Don't see dull days as unsuitable for photography–just think of them as black and white days!

324 Check the weather forecast

If you're planning a long trip or a really early start, it's always worth checking the long-term weather forecast for the area you intend to visit–just search the internet for a list of local websites. That said, don't be afraid to chance your arm –"bad" weather can produce amazing landscapes.

325 Use a tripod

They're a hassle to carry around, but a tripod is vital for successful landscape photography, allowing you to fine-tune a composition, leave the camera in position while waiting for the light to improve, and to keep the camera steady so you can use long exposure in low light.

326 Get to know a location

Initial visits to a location often result in unoriginal pictures, but if you keep going back you will get to know the area more intimately and see beyond the obvious. Go back at different times of day, different seasons, and in a variety of weather conditions.

327 On your doorstep

There's a lot to be said for exploring your own backyard, wherever you live, you're sure to find interesting locations close to home that you can get to at short notice when the light's good, instead of having to plan trips in advance and travel long distances.

328 Quality of light

The quality of light is the one thing that can make or break a great color landscape. It doesn't matter how amazing the scene is or how dramatic your composition, if the light's flat and drab then your photographs will be too.

329 On the road

When traveling with your camera to foreign countries, try to research in advance the quality of the light at different times of day. For example, the sun will set very quickly in the tropics, but in temperate regions during the summer the sun will take a long time to set.

330 Warm light

Early and late in the day when the sun is low in the sky, the light has a beautiful natural warmth that brings the landscape to life and produces images full of atmosphere and good feeling.

331 Cold light

In stormy, cold, or misty weather, the light has a natural coolness to it that adds an eerie, mysterious feel to landscapes. This is most pronounced when shooting in the shade where the light is even cooler. Also, try using long exposures at twilight to create cool images.

333 Hard light

Direct sunlight is hard and harsh, casting strong shadows and creating bright highlights. The higher the sun is in the sky, the harder the light—so high summer sees the light at its hardest. While unsuitable for general landscape photography, such conditions can be effective for more abstract images.

332 Soft light

Soft light is ideal for revealing fine detail and tone in the landscape, because contrast is very low and there are no hard shadows or shimmering highlights to deal with. Cloudy weather produces this kind of light, or stepping into the shade when the sun is shining. Predawn and after sunset the light is also soft and atmospheric.

334 Shooting sunrise and sunset

Sunrise and sunset are prime times for landscape photography—especially near water, which reflects the warmth of the sun and sky. Use your longest telephoto or zoom lens to enlarge the sun's orb—taking precautions if the sun is bright to protect your eyes—and silhouette bold shapes such as boats, trees, and buildings.

336 Silhouettes

Silhouettes make great landscape subjects. The best way to photograph them is to expose for the highlights, rendering the darker areas underexposed. Try to get an even balance between dark and light areas so that the silhouette doesn't completely overpower the picture.

337 Rainbows

Rainbows are formed when the sun shines through falling rain, adding a welcome splash of color to otherwise dark, brooding landscapes. Turn your back to the sun in such conditions to check for one.

335 Storm light

The most dramatic conditions for landscape photography often occur when the sun breaks through a dark, stormy sky, so don't be too keen to head for cover at the first sign of bad weather. Stormy light is most likely on blustery days, when dark clouds are scudding across the sky and momentarily obscure the sun.

338 Mist and fog

Mist and fog reduce the landscape to a series of soft tones and two-dimensional shapes. Emphasize the effect using a telephoto or zoom lens and concentrate on cold features such as trees or buildings. River views also look beautiful in misty weather—especially at sunrise, when the warmth of the sun slowly burns the mist away.

339 Lighting direction

The direction a scene is lit from by the sun will have a strong influence on the mood of the final image, so always give this some thought when composing landscapes.

340 From the side

With the sun off to one side of the camera, the landscape is side lit, so shadows fall across the scene and texture and form are revealed. This is the most effective lighting for landscapes, especially early or late in the day when the sun is low in the sky.

341 From the front

If you shoot with the sun to your back, the scene will be frontally lit so shadows fall away from the camera. Frontal lighting can be effective, especially when the light is warm, but the resulting photographs can look rather flat.

342 Back to front

Shooting into the light, or contre-jour, produces striking results. In strong light, bold features in the scene will record as silhouettes—a handy technique at sunrise and sunset—while in stormy weather you can capture amazing cloudburst effects. Shadows rush toward the camera, which can look stunning when shooting woodland scenes. Watch for flare, and be aware that underexposure is likely.

343 Rivers and streams

Rivers and streams make great lead-in lines that help carry the eye through a composition. On misty mornings they look incredibly atmospheric and at sunrise and sunset will mirror the fiery colors in the sky.

344 Time it right

Although landscape photography is a slow and contemplative subject, there can still be a "decisive moment" when all the elements in a scene come together, so don't get too laid back, or you might miss it.

345 Include reflections

Reflections add an extra dimension to landscapes, so on calm days head for flat water. Fill the foreground of your pictures with a reflection of the scene beyond, or use a telezoom lens to concentrate on parts of the reflection to create striking abstract images.

346 Shadowplay

Shadows not only help to reveal texture and form in the landscape but they can also be a useful compositional aid. For example, when the sun is low in the sky, use the shadows of trees as lead-in lines, and hide your own shadow by standing in the shadow of a tree.

347 Shooting in snow

Snow tends to fool camera meters into underexposure, so be prepared to dial in anything from +1 to +2 stops to compensate.

348 The harder you work

You can't take great landscapes from the comfort of your armchair, so get out there into the great outdoors, put your best foot forward, and explore.

How to photograph...

Architecture and urban landscape

Big, small, old, new, grand, modest, traditional, cutting edge–buildings come in all shapes and forms, and all make great photographic subjects.

349 Verticals

If you photograph a tall building from close range with a wide-angle lens you will have no option but to tilt the camera back to get the top of the building in-frame. This results in converging verticals, where the sides of the building lean inward, and the building appears to be toppling over.

350 Avoiding converging verticals

The easiest way to avoid converging verticals is to keep your camera back square to the subject building–any unwanted foreground can be cropped out later. Other options are to back away and use a longer lens, or shoot from a slightly higher vantage point, a wall or a stepladder, for example.

351 Correcting converging verticals in-camera

A shift lens, also known as a Perspective Control (PC) lens, is designed to avoid converging verticals by allowing you to adjust the front elements of the lens so you can include the top of a building while keeping the camera back square. Alternatively, download the image onto the computer and correct the converging verticals using image-editing software. It's a simple, routine task.

352 Exploit converging verticals

Of course, you don't have to get rid of converging verticals–instead, why not make a feature of the effect by shooting buildings from ground level with your widest lens?

353 Time of day

A building's aspect will influence the best time of day to photograph it, so use a compass to establish which way it faces and time your shoot accordingly.

354 Shooting skylines

Cities often look their best when captured from a distance, as you can capture their true grandeur without the traffic, crowds, and congestion. Views across water are especially effective because the skyline will be reflected.

356 Reflected glory

You can take great shots of buildings reflected in other nearby buildings—industrial estates and business parks are great places to do this, as modern buildings with huge windows are constructed close together. Make sure the sun is shining on the building caught in the reflection.

357 Exterior details

Use a telezoom lens to isolate interesting architectural details—old buildings such as cathedrals and castles can be great sources of such elements.

355 Twilight zone

Twilight is often the best time to shoot towering modern architecture because the sky acts like a huge diffuser, softening the light so contrast is low while the pastel colors in the sky are mirrored by any reflective surfaces in the building.

358 Perfect symmetry

Symmetry makes for eye-catching compositions, so keep a look out for examples when exploring the urban landscape. Many modern buildings are highly symmetrical in their designs, while reflections can create symmetry by mirroring architectural features.

359 Go for graphics

Modern buildings tend to be very graphic, making use of bold shapes, strong lines, hard edges, and repetition. In bright sunlight against blue sky these features make perfect abstract images.

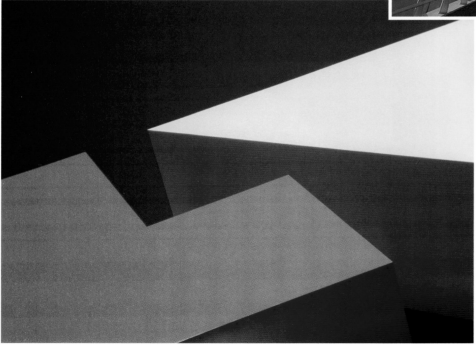

360 Early riser

By 8am most big towns and cities are already bustling with traffic and people, so if you want to avoid the noise and crowds make sure you're on location at first light when the streets are empty.

361 Night views

The urban landscape is often at its most stunning once the sun sets, light levels fade, and manmade illumination takes over. The best time to shoot night scenes is while there is still color in the sky, as this will provide an attractive backdrop while details will still be visible in the shadows.

362 Unusual reflections

Towns and cities are full of unusual reflections—in polished surfaces, wet paintwork, puddles, pools—so instead of just shooting an interesting subject or scene, capture a reflection of it instead to give your pictures a novel twist.

363 Contrast old with new

Towns and cities evolve over the centuries, so changes in architectural trends through the ages can often be seen side by side. This contrast of the old and the new can result in fascinating photographs— for example, an ancient stone church reflecting in the glass panels of a modern office block.

364 Window on the world

Windows make a great subject in their own right. You can use them to frame the view outside or capture reflections, while the rich colors in stained glass can be the source of stunning shots.

365 Heavy industry

Bridges, cranes, and other examples of heavy industry make great subjects— especially at night when they're often illuminated by colorful floodlights, or when captured in silhouette against the rising or setting sun.

366 Inside jobs

Buildings are often more interesting inside than out—especially older buildings—so don't forget to take a look inside when you've finished shooting the exterior.

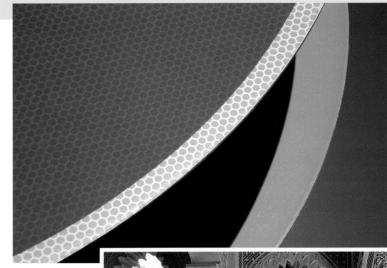

367 Sign of the times

Our towns and cities are full of signs that make great subjects. Neon signs outside bars and clubs are best photographed at night, while colorful road signs look great in strong sunlight captured against blue sky. Move in close to photograph parts of the sign and create striking abstract images.

368 Numbers game

Numbers make a great photographic theme, and towns and cities are full of them—on doors, painted on walls, printed on vehicles. Why not shoot a set of images of the numbers one to 100 and see how many different styles and designs you can find?

369 Alternative angles

Turn everyday urban subjects into stunning images by shooting them from unusual angles. For example, look skyward while standing beneath an electricity pylon, or look down from the top of a spiral staircase.

370 Streaked lighting

To create streaks of light from moving cars, set the camera on a tripod, manually focus the lens, and set an exposure of between 10 sec and 20 sec at f/22. Use the Bulb (Time) setting if necessary, and activate the shutter using a cable release.

371 Down your street

You don't have to go far to discover interesting urban subjects—a stroll down your own street will reveal all kinds of things, from architectural details to graffiti. It's not what you shoot, but how you shoot it, and, if you can overcome familiarity, your own neighborhood can be hugely inspiring.

372 Create an architectural montage

You will have seen posters for sale showing local architectural details—doors and windows are popular as they vary so much. Why not work on a similar project yourself then combine the images in Photoshop to create a montage?

373 Photographing markets

Markets are great haunts for photographers. There are endless candid opportunities, of market traders as well as the general public, and markets are packed with interesting colors, details, and patterns.

374 Cityscapes

City buildings lit at night can be photographed close-up or as part of a wider scene. Light from the buildings should mean that AF works effectively. Exposures will vary from around 2 sec at f/11 for a tightly cropped scene, or 8 sec at f/11 so that the city forms part of a wider landscape. Cityscapes often look best when photographed from a high vantage point, such as from a balcony on a tall building or from a high, distant hill. If buildings are floodlit and photographed with a tight crop, increase the shutter speed to -1 sec.

How to photograph...

People

We all shoot pictures of people, but how many of them could be regarded as true portraits?

375 Lenses for portraits

The ideal lens for traditional head-and-shoulders portraits is said to be a short telephoto of around 100 to 105mm, as this will compress perspective a little, which flatters facial features.

376 Set AE to aperture priority

To obscure distracting background clutter, select aperture-priority AE mode, and set a large aperture (around f/2.8 or f/4). The resulting lack of depth of field will cause background detail to appear blurred, helping to isolate and draw attention to your subject.

377 Check the whole viewfinder

Make sure you check all areas of the viewfinder to identify any distracting objects in the foreground, at the edges of the frame, or in the background. Remember that most DSLR cameras have a viewfinder with only 93-95 percent coverage, so some areas of the scene that will appear on the image won't be seen through the viewfinder.

378 Capturing character

The aim of portraiture is to try to capture the character of your sitter. Sounds easy, but to do it well you need patience and the ability to communicate with your subject so they reveal their true self to the camera. Watch for any candid moments when your subject shows emotion through facial expressions, such as laughter or a mischievous look. Have the camera ready to point and shoot with a wide aperture and fast shutter speed set to ensure you capture the moment with no image blur. Crop tightly around the face and head, using a short telephoto lens or zoom setting, to maximize the impact of the expression.

379 Filling the frame

In a portrait the subject should generally take center stage. Make sure they do that by filling the frame and excluding any unwanted details that will only serve to distract the viewer.

380 Where should the eyes be?

It's tempting to put a person's eyes in the middle of the picture, but the composition will look more balanced and interesting if they're roughly a third of the way down from the top of the frame.

382 Revealing texture

The best way to reveal texture in a person's skin is by lighting them from the side so one half of the face is lit and the other half is thrown into shadow. This is great for character portraits but isn't always particularly flattering!

383 Hiding skin blemishes

To hide spots, wrinkles, and other skin blemishes, avoid side lighting and instead flood your subject's face with soft light so there are no visible shadows. Overcast weather or open shade is ideal as the light will be soft. Reflectors can also be used to bounce light into the shadows.

381 Adding catch lights

Catch lights help to put a sparkle in your subject's eyes. You can create them using fill-in flash when shooting outdoors or by holding a reflector near the camera. In the studio, brollies or softboxes fitted over the lights will create perfect catch lights.

384 Flattery will get you everywhere

Many people hate being photographed, so the least you can do is try and make them look good!

- Hide bald patches in men by shooting from a slightly lower position so the top of your subject's head can't be seen.
- Conceal double chins by shooting slightly higher then normal so your subject has to look up–this stretches the neck a little.
- Long noses are best tackled head on–side views merely make them appear longer.
- Avoid using lenses shorter than 100mm from close range as they exaggerate facial features.

385 Candid camera

Most people become guarded when they see a camera pointing at them, so the easiest way to capture natural expressions and true emotions is by shooting candidly to make sure your subject isn't aware of the camera. You'll need a telephoto lens (ideally about 200mm), or a high magnification zoom (around 5x-10x), so that you don't impose on the subject and spoil the unposed effect. You should, however, seek permission from your subject with this sort of picture.

386 People at work

Photographing people at work is a great way to shoot character portraits. We also tend to feel more relaxed in our natural environment—our comfort zone—so you stand a better chance of taking natural, revealing portraits. Why not take your camera to your own place of work and shoot a series of portraits of your colleagues?

387 Beware of shadows

When photographing people outdoors in bright, overhead sunlight, unflattering shadows are likely to form under the forehead, nose, and chin. This is particularly true with a point-and-shoot approach to photography. If it's impossible to move your subject to a different spot with softer lighting, then use the pop-up flash on the camera (or an external flash unit) to add some fill-in flash, which will lighten the shadow areas.

388 Poser's guide

Professional models know exactly how to strike a pose that makes them look good. Unfortunately, the rest of us tend to turn into waxworks the minute a camera points at us, so you will need to give your subject some help if you want to take natural, relaxed portraits.

389 Subject standing

Standing poses can work, but only if your subject is confident. Help them along by suggesting that they put their hands in their pockets or rest one hand on a hip. Asking your subject to stand side on to the camera then turn their head to face it can also work.

390 Subject sitting

Asking your subject to sit down will immediately make them feel more relaxed. Also, we all have a certain way of sitting that helps to reveal our personalities.

391 Children as subjects

Children can get easily bored so you'll need to keep them entertained in some way if you want to hold their attention (although a picture of a bored child can have a charm of its own).

392 Hands

When being photographed, people are often at a loss as to what to do with their hands, which end up looking unnatural. Check whether the hands look natural. If not, then get your subject to relax and see where the hands fall—this is usually the best place for them. Alternatively, give your model something to hold.

Make sure the hands are in a natural pose.

393 Formal poses

For more formal, posed portraits, ask your subject to sit in a chair with their back straight. Instead of shooting head on, turn the chair 45 degrees then ask your subject to turn their head and face the camera.

396 Dynamic poses

If your subject is confident in front of the camera you can really go to town. Ask them to strike a sequence of unusual poses and fire away as they do so. Shooting from a low viewpoint or leaning the camera slightly to one side will also make the composition more dynamic.

397 Parts of the body

Portraits don't always have to show faces, why not concentrate on parts of the body instead–hands, for example, can be a fascinating subject because they tell us so much about a person.

394 Hands cupping face

A classic pose for a seated subject is to have them rest their face on cupped hands. It's a natural and relaxed pose, although make sure the sitter doesn't slouch and that the shape of their face isn't distorted. Alternatively, resting the head against one hand also looks attractive and comfortable as it's a pose we often adopt when relaxing.

395 Focus on the eyes

The eyes are said to be the windows of the soul, so always focus on your subject's eyes. If the end of the nose or the tips of the ears are out of focus it doesn't matter, but if the eyes aren't sharp then a portrait will fail because they are the first element we look at.

398 Framing

You can focus attention on your subject by placing them within their own frame, such as a door or window. Compositionally, this technique works in the same way that framing a photographic print makes the print look better. Natural frames outdoors are overhanging branches of a tree, an archway, or similar object.

Framing your subject will improve the composition.

399 Advanced lighting effects

Rather than the standard approach to lighting, photograph your subject with the sun behind them to create rim lighting or a silhouette. For rim lighting, avoid having the sun directly in the picture, and expose for the subject. You will need to use the spot-metering mode and take your meter reading from the subject. For a silhouette effect, set the exposure for the highlights by framing the scene with just the sky visible in the viewfinder. Then, use the AE-Lock button or function to lock the exposure before reframing the scene with your subject in the picture.

400 Outdoor lighting

Avoid photographing your subject in direct sunlight in the middle of the day. An overcast day will produce a better quality of light for subtle skin tones with no harsh shadows. For an image with more contrast, but maintaining nice lighting, I recommend photographing in the early morning on a clear day.

How to photograph...

Still life

Whether you shoot things as they're found or build your own pictures, still-life photography can result in amazing images and test your skills to the limit.

Creating still lifes

Still-life photography may seem like a tough subject because you start off with a blank canvas rather than a full one, but this is what makes it challenging and rewarding—you're creating photographs from nothing.

 Keep it simple

Simplicity is the key to great still-life photography. Just work with one or two items and see what you can produce.

403 Watch the background

The background you use can make or break a great still life, so think about what you use. Natural and textured materials will enhance natural objects, while simple, plain backgrounds such as paper or card are a better choice when you want your subject to take center stage.

404 Leave it out

Don't be afraid to let some of the props in your still life break out of the edges of the frame—the composition will be more interesting than if you arrange everything neatly in the center.

405 Revealing texture

If you want to reveal texture in an object, light it from the side. You can do this with windowlight, but for more control try using a reading lamp or, better still, a slide projector, and adjust the white balance on your camera to get rid of any unwanted color cast from the light source.

409 Stick to a theme

Working to a theme can help to focus your ideas because it limits your range of subject matter, and often one picture naturally leads to another. The theme could be a color, a subject, a particular object—anything you like.

410 Found still lifes

If creating your own still lifes doesn't appeal, why not go in search of found still lifes instead and shoot things as you discover them. Old buildings, junk yards, greenhouses, beaches, and construction sites are great places to find interesting objects in situ.

406 Windowlight will do

You don't need fancy studio lights to produce successful still lifes—windowlight is perfectly adequate, and it can be controlled using reflectors, or modified with masks to reduce the amount of light, or softened with diffusing screens made from tracing paper or sheer material.

407 Using color

Color could be the basis of your still-life shots—then all you have to do is find suitable props. Go for contrasting colors—such as yellow/blue and green/red—or juxtapose objects to create color harmony by concentrating on warm hues, cold hues, or soft, muted colors

408 Household objects

If you look around your home you'll find all kinds of subject matter for still lifes—collections of coins, medals, or old toys; plants and flower arrangements; cutlery; kids' toys; even small things like colored paperclips and thumbtacks. It's not what you shoot but how you shoot it.

How to photograph...

Macro and close-up

Macro photography allows you to explore a whole new world—one that's often far more interesting than what we can see with the naked eye.

Shooting close-ups

Although many zoom lenses have a macro facility, they generally don't allow you to shoot true macro images, which have a reproduction ratio of lifesize (1:1) or greater. To do that you'll need either a real macro lens or, alternatively, extension tubes or bellows.

412 Reversing rings

A cheap and easy way to shoot macro images is to use a reversing ring—this screws onto the front of your lens and allows you to mount it on the camera back to front so it focuses really close. Some functions such as autoexposure and autofocus will be lost.

413 Make the ordinary extraordinary

By going in really close you can turn everyday objects into fascinating images. Think of the patterns of veins and cells in a leaf or the tiny grains of pollen in a flower. Literally anything can be the source of a great photograph.

414 Patterns in nature

Mother Nature provides us with an endless range of subjects for close-up photography. Your own garden will be full of opportunities—from the detail in tree bark to lichens on rocks and stones, flowers, grasses, leaves, fungi, and much more.

415 Create your own subject

Why not try creating your own close-up still lifes? A great technique to try is placing things in a tray of water then letting it freeze—flowers, leaves, and berries are ideal.

416 As simple as that

Keep your close-up compositions simple. Concentrate on one key subject and make sure the background is uncluttered so it doesn't compete for attention—you can replace a natural background with a plain sheet of card if necessary.

417 Focus carefully

Critical focusing is essential when shooting close-ups because depth of field is minimal. The slightest change can throw your subject out of focus. Manual focus is by far the best and most accurate means of focusing the lens during macro photography. Use the focus indicator light in the viewfinder to confirm that the camera has focused the lens before pressing the shutter.

418 Maximize depth of field

To maximize depth of field, stop your lens down to its smallest aperture–usually f/22 or f/32 with macro lenses. Even then, the zone of sharp focus will be just a fraction of an inch if you're shooting at lifesize or greater.

420 Use depth of field preview

If your camera has a depth of field preview button, use it to assess how much of the area in front of and behind the point of focus appears sharp.

421 Keep steady

It's much easier to achieve perfect focus if your camera is mounted on a tripod so that it doesn't move. Handholding is possible, but the slightest movement may throw your subject out of focus.

419 Minimize depth of field

You can produce some great effects by shooting with your lens at its widest aperture–which minimizes depth of field–so only a very narrow zone of sharp focus is achieved while everything else is blurred beyond recognition.

422 Put your subject in the shade

Harsh sunlight is generally unsuitable for close-ups. If you can't move your subject into the shade, create your own by holding a large sheet of card over it. White card doubles as a handy reflector.

423 Flash of inspiration

Using flash for close-ups solves numerous problems—the burst of light will freeze any movement, so you can work at smaller apertures to maximize what little depth of field there is, and the flash will provide even illumination in the shadiest spots

424 Mirror lock

One of the great things about close-up photography is you can practice it no matter what the weather's like. On rainy days you can either set up shots indoors using windowlight as illumination, or work outdoors under a large umbrella—as well as keeping the rain off it will also act as a diffuser and soften the light.

425 Rainy-day close-ups

It's a good idea to use your camera's mirror lock-up when shooting close-ups so that vibrations are minimized when you trip the shutter—even the slightest vibration can reduce image sharpness.

426 Flower power

Flowers are perfect subjects for close-up photography because they not only offer endless photographic options, from portraits to abstracts, but they are also available in a wide range of varieties and colors and can be photographed all year round, indoors and out.

427 The beauty of backlighting

Backlighting is a great way to reveal the colors and patterns in translucent subjects. Leaves are a common example, but spiders' webs, butterflies' wings, and many other natural subjects look their best when lit from behind.

428 Background detail

Using flash at close quarters is likely to result in an underexposed background, rendering it almost black. This is OK for isolating the subject and for emphasizing certain features, such as line or shape; however, it looks unnatural. To brighten the background, set the camera to slow-sync flash mode, which will allow more of the ambient light to register on the sensor.

429 Photographing texture

The world is full of fascinating textures—both natural and manmade—and the closer you look the more interesting they get. As well as obvious things such as tree bark, moss, and rocks, look at things like fish scales, blades of grass, sand, wood grain, skin, and fabrics.

430 What is it?

Why not photograph a selection of household objects close-up and see if your family can guess what they are? Kitchen implements, sponges, toothbrushes, and other everyday items can be used. You'll be surprised how different they look.

431 Just add water

Spraying flowers and plants with a mist of water will coat them in tiny droplets that sparkle in the light and add to the overall effect. Plant misters are ideal for this.

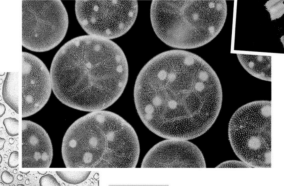

432 Macro subjects

The macro world is hidden from our everyday view of nature and the environment—that's what makes it so exciting. Texture, patterns, shapes, and colors all make fascinating macro subjects, which will reveal to you and your friends worlds previously unseen.

How to photograph...

Nature and wildlife

From garden creatures to big game, the world is full of fascinating wildlife—and all of it makes for great photography.

433 Using long lenses

Wild animals and birds are generally very cautious creatures, so to get frame-filling pictures you're going to need a long telephoto lens—300mm is about the minimum, but 400mm or even 600mm would be better.

434 Add a teleconverter

If a long telephoto lens is beyond your budget, then a teleconverter is a less expensive alternative. This accessory fits between your lens and your camera, and increases its effective focal length by a given multiplication factor, usually 1.5x, 1.7x, 2x, or 3x. For example, a 200mm lens with a 2x converter would have a focal length of 400mm. However, remember you will lose a stop or so of exposure.

435 Blur the background

Use a wide lens aperture—possibly the widest your lens has—to minimize depth of field, so your subject is isolated from the background.

436 Fill the frame for impact

The most impressive wildlife pictures are those where the main subject fills the frame and makes the viewer feel that they're right there, up close and personal.

437 Set shutter-priority for action

To capture action shots of animals with fine detail, set the AE mode to shutter-priority and select a fast shutter speed (about 1/500 sec or faster). Pan the camera to follow the movement of the animal.

438 Use the ISO control for faster shutter speeds

If the light level is too low to enable setting a fast shutter speed, even with the aperture wide open, then consider increasing the sensitivity of the sensor using the ISO control. Increasing ISO from 100 to 400 will give you two extra stops of light to play with, potentially changing a shutter speed of 1/125 sec to 1/500 sec.

439 A sense of motion

Alternatively, for a greater sense of motion, select a shutter speed of about 1/30 sec to create speed blur, which adds to the atmosphere of a picture. Pan the camera to follow the movement of the animal.

440 Set AF to continuous

To keep the subject in focus, set the AF mode to continuous servo (AI-servo) to enable the camera to track the movement of the animal, and adjust the focus point accordingly. This is particularly helpful when photographing birds in flight

441 Shooting from a hide

A good way to get close to timid wildlife is to erect a hide in an area where animals or birds are frequent visitors. Don't expect instant success, though–it may take many visits before you get the right shots.

442 The point of focus

It's important when photographing animals to focus on the eyes. Select continuous AF mode with wide-area AF to increase the likelihood of the camera focusing on the right point. Make sure that the active AF sensor is covering the eye. Alternatively, with stationary animals, switch to manual focus and do it yourself.

443 Depth of field

Extensive depth of field is less critical in wildlife photography than in, say, landscape, but you will need enough depth of field to ensure the eyes and nose appear sharp. When using telephoto lenses, this becomes more difficult to achieve. In general, an aperture 2- to 3-stops closed from maximum (e.g. f/5.6-f/8 on an f/2.8 lens) will be sufficient.

444 Knowing your subject

Successful wildlife photographers are also nature lovers who study their subjects, get to know the habits and habitats of their quarry, and are prepared to spend hour after hour just watching and waiting. You should never disturb animals with young, and always return any environment you've disturbed to its natural state. If an animal appears agitated then slowly and quietly move away. Many countries have laws that extend to wildlife and the countryside, and you should make sure you are aware of them before venturing out.

445 Stalking your prey

If you want to achieve success when stalking wild animals, make sure you dress in drab or camouflage clothing, cover up any shiny or reflective surfaces on your camera and lenses, avoid wearing perfume, aftershave, or deodorants, and always stay downwind of your prey.

Animals in zoos

446 Zoo animals

Zoos and safari parks are easily accessible for animal photography. Beware of background distractions (e.g. people, cars, fences) that detract from the "natural look" of the image. Check the picture on the LCD screen after taking to make sure you haven't caught any unwanted detail.

447 Perspective

Animals rarely look good when photographed from above. Get low down and photograph them at eye-level whenever possible. This will produce a far more engaging composition and natural perspective.

448 Take a macro lens

You can get much closer to animals in captivity than you can in the wild. Change your usual lens for a macro lens, and focus your attention on the fine detail, such as patterns on fur, the eyes, paws, and so on.

449 Shooting through wire

Choose a telephoto lens and set the aperture to its maximum setting (largest hole). Hold the camera parallel to, and right against, the fence, with the center of the lens pointing through the hole in the wire. In most cases, the wire will appear so far out of focus you won't see it at all.

450 Turn off the flash to photograph through glass

If your camera has a pop-up flash, it may automatically activate in low-light conditions, such as when photographing indoors. If you are trying to photograph through glass, the flash will bounce of the glass and produce flare, spoiling your picture. Turn the auto-flash off in the menu settings, if your camera allows it.

451 When to press the shutter

When is it the right time to press the shutter? This is a question every photographer asks. Here's a little trick to help you decide. When looking through the viewfinder at the scene, ask your self the question: "How would I caption this photo?" If the only caption you can think of is the species name, then the picture probably isn't worth taking. Look for actions, behavior, and expressions (humor, interaction, bonding, etc.) that capture the essence of the subject.

452 On safari

The ultimate in wildlife photography has to be shooting big game in exotic locations–so start saving! There are many specialist companies that organize guided photo safaris in Africa, Latin America, and India.

453 Your own backyard

Of course, you don't have to travel across the world to take great wildlife pictures– many species of animals and birds frequent gardens, parks, and even urban areas.

454 Keep the camera steady

Long lenses increase the risk of camera shake, so if you're using one, try to support it whenever possible. Walls, fallen trees, posts, and other natural supports are ideal, and a beanbag will provide a cushion to keep the lens steady.

How to photograph...

Sport and action

Whether it's the Super Bowl or a game of soccer in your local park, the skills required to compose great action shots are the same.

455 Know the rules

The key to success in sports or action photography is to know your subject well enough to be able to predict what's likely to happen next and keep up with the action. Anticipating the shot will go a long way to making sure that parts of your subject aren't lost out of frame.

456 Everyday action

You don't need to visit major sporting venues to take great action shots. Everyday action–kids racing around on their bicycles or running along the beach, for example–can make great pictures.

457 Camera panning

To freeze the action in some sports, such as motor racing and speedway, try following the movement of the subject with the camera–a technique known as panning–and press the shutter partway through the movement. Keep panning after taking the shot to avoid a sudden stop causing camera shake and image blur.

Use the camera panning technique for clear images of fast moving subjects.

458 Freezing movement

The single most important factor determining whether or not you freeze a moving subject is the shutter speed, and the one you need depends on how fast your subject is moving, how far away it is from the camera, and the direction it's moving in relation to the camera. Here's a list of suggested speeds for common subjects:

Subject	Across path Full frame	Across path Half frame	Head on
Jogger	1/250sec.	1/125sec.	1/60sec.
Sprinter	1/500sec.	1/250sec.	1/125sec.
Cyclist	1/500sec.	1/250sec.	1/125sec.
Trotting horse	1/250sec.	1/125sec.	1/60sec.
Galloping horse	1/1000sec.	1/500sec.	1/250sec.
Tennis serve	1/1000sec.	1/500sec.	1/250sec.
Car at 40mph (65kmph)	1/500sec.	1/250sec.	1/125sec.
Car at 70mph (110kmph)	1/1000sec.	1/500sec.	1/250sec.
Train	1/2000sec.	1/1000sec.	1/500sec.

459 Eye-level action

Getting down to pitch level is a better option. Watch the action for a while and see if you can pick up on specific trends (such as the line taken by racing cars, horses in a steeplechase, or cyclists on a mountain climb), and then get yourself in the right position to photograph the action.

460 Account for shutter lag

When you trip the camera's shutter to take a picture there's a fractional delay before the shutter opens. With fast-moving subjects this delay can make or break a great shot, so remember to fire just before the crucial moment.

461 Tracking your subject

The only way to take successful action shots of moving subjects that don't follow a predictable path is by following them with the camera so you can shoot at the decisive moment. To keep your subject in sharp focus as you track it, set the autofocus to Predictive or Servo mode.

462 Shoot a sequence

Sequences of action pictures can often be more telling and dramatic than single frames, so don't be afraid to set your camera's motordrive to Continuous and keep your finger on the shutter to expose several frames in quick succession.

463 Practice makes perfect

Photographing sport and action is perhaps the hardest photographic job you'll encounter because you need fast reflexes and perfect timing. Initially your hit rate will probably be low, but the more you practice the better you'll become.

464 Go wide

Although telephoto lenses are the mainstay of sport and action photographers, you can get stunning pictures by moving in really close with a wide-angle lens. Events such as marathons, fun runs, and city center cycling are ideal for this technique because you can get close to your subject. BMX stunt biking and skateboarding are other subjects worth shooting with wide lenses.

465 Use blur creatively

Action pictures don't have to be sharp. In fact, in many cases some creative blur will actually produce a more effective image, so experiment with slow shutter speeds when photographing everyday moving subjects and see what happens.

466 Watch the background

Sporting venues are often littered with advertising hoardings that can make the background very distracting. The same applies if you're shooting toward crowds of spectators. To avoid problems, find a vantage point where the background is less cluttered. Failing that, shoot with your lens at its widest aperture to minimize depth of field, or pan the camera so the background blurs.

467 Unusual angles

Try shooting popular sports from unusual angles. Place your camera on the ground so it's pointing up, for example, or find a high viewpoint so you're looking down. You could also set shots up—maybe laying on the ground and asking your subject to jump over you so you can capture them with a wide-angle lens against the sky.

You need to anticipate the action for good sports photography.

468 Get in position

Try to get a good vantage point to photograph from, where your view is not obscured by spectators or other obstructions. For example, trying to photograph a baseball game from the stand will generally mean having to shoot through an exuberant crowd when anything exciting happens.

469 Use a zoom lens

A zoom lens with a range of between 100-400mm enables you to select the best composition without having to continually relocate your position, which can be difficult or impossible at some events.

How to photograph...

Vacations and travel

From family vacations to global adventures, our travels expose us to a myriad of fascinating and often exotic subjects. Here's how to do them justice.

470 Do your homework

It's worth researching your holiday destination to assess its photographic potential. Just do an Internet search on the place and see what comes up, or enter the destination into the search engine of a picture library's website and check out the images that come up. The more you know about a place before you get there, the less time you'll waste when you arrive.

471 Check out the postcards

Postcards are always a good indication of the most popular subjects and scenes in a location, so check them out as soon as you can and buy a selection to use as visual reminders.

472 Make the most of light

Early morning and evening are the best times of day for travel photography—not only because the light quality is high but also because there are fewer tourists around to spoil the view.

473 Less is more

When you're traveling, everything seems new, different, and exciting, and it's tempting to photograph everything in sight. However, if you do that you'll be disappointed with most of the pictures, so try to resist and think carefully about each shot you take.

474 The road less traveled

When on vacation, we tend to think of sandy beaches and historic buildings and monuments as subjects for our photos. Don't limit your photography to the obvious. Attach a wide-range zoom lens (e.g. 28-200mm) and head into the markets, or wander down the out-of-the-way side streets for photographic inspiration.

475 Candid camera

People do the most wonderful (or craziest) things when they think no one is looking. Watch out for those special moments and have your camera ready to capture the scene. This might be a time for point-and-shoot photography.

476 Shooting famous monuments

Famous monuments—the Empire State Building or the Eiffel Tower, for instance—have been photographed millions of times, so if you are going to shoot these, try to come up with something original. Visit early or late in the day when there a fewer people around, experiment with unusual camera angles, use extra-long or extra-wide lenses, shoot panoramas...

477 Avoiding the clichés

It's hard to avoid shooting clichés when traveling because they present themselves at every turn. However, if you get them out of the way as soon as you arrive you can then concentrate on producing original work.

478 Life's a beach

Tropical beach scenes are irresistible to photographers because they're symbolic of so many things–tranquillity, paradise, escape, etc. Shoot them in the middle of the day–a time when many tourists will have retreated to the shade to escape the heat, so leaving the scene clearer for you. The overhead sun will make the sand shimmer, and the sea will reflect the blue sky and look amazing.

479 Capture symbolic details

Small details can say as much about the character of a place as grand views or famous monuments. They're also often far more interesting photographically because they're less corny.

480 Put people in the picture

Local people give a place its character as much as the buildings and landscape, so don't be afraid to shoot a few portraits during your travels. If you ask permission rather than trying to grab shots, you'll be surprised just how responsive people are to being photographed.

481 The earth from the air

Make the most of an airplane flight by taking some pictures from the airplane's window. Select a wide aperture and set focus to infinity. Keep the lens parallel with, and close to, the window, to avoid reflections and glare. Be aware of the wings, but don't necessarily exclude them—they can add a sense of place. At very high altitude, fit a UV filter to the lens to reduce the amount of UV light entering the camera.

482 Composition

Include foreground objects to add interest. Emphasize leading lines that draw the viewer into the picture space. Change camera angle and perspective to alter the relationship between objects and pictorial elements.

483 Beat the crowds

Rise early to avoid the crowds at popular destinations. Most visitors to the main attractions arrive and leave during the middle of the day. Waking early will reward you with crowd-free scenes and great photographic light.

484 Photography in public places

The world is getting warier, and what used to be an accepted aspect of travel culture (e.g. vacation photos) has, in some places, become a reason for over-zealous officialdom. Beware of photographing any child who isn't your own, and expect at some landmarks to be accosted by a fellow in a uniform with a clipboard. Unless threatened with arrest (or a gun), never hand over your camera or memory cards to anyone.

How to photograph...

Night and low light

Photographs taken at night or in low light can be strikingly atmospheric, but there are a few things that you should consider to get the best results.

485 Preprogrammed night exposure modes

Beware of using the camera's preprogrammed night-exposure modes. They will give acceptable results in general situations, but may not always be suitable for what you're trying to achieve. Even when using these settings, always use a tripod to minimize the likelihood of camera shake.

486 Use the Bulb (Time) shutter-speed setting

DSLR cameras have a shutter-speed setting known as Bulb or Time. This setting enables shutter speeds in excess of the camera's preset maximum (usually around 30 sec) up to several minutes or hours. Use this setting when very long exposures are necessary.

487 Beware of noise

During very long exposures, the build-up of noise may be so great that the noise reduction function is only partially successful at removing it.

488 Increasing ISO (sensitivity)

If it's so dark that you're struggling to get a workable exposure, increase the sensitivity of the sensor using the ISO control. A shutter speed of 8 sec can be reduced to 1/2 sec by changing the ISO setting from 100 to 1600. But be aware that high ISO settings will introduce noise to the final result.

489 The advantage of fast lenses

The faster the lens (that is the wider the aperture) the more control you will have over exposure settings. For example, a lens with a maximum aperture of f/2 is 3-stops faster than a lens with a maximum aperture of f/5.6. These three stops can turn a noise-generating shutter speed of 2 sec to a more acceptable 1/4 sec.

490 Focusing in the dark

Autofocus is less efficient at night, particularly those systems that use contrast detection to assess subject distance. The lack of contrast in low light often causes AF to go into hunt mode. Look for a bright area of the scene close to your main subject, such as a street lamp or a lit window, and use that as the point of focus. If that fails to solve troublesome AF, switch to manual focus mode.

492 Moonlight

When using moonlight as the main light source, set a shutter speed of around 4min when the moon is full and the sky clear. Double the amount of exposure when the moon is partial. To photograph the moon itself, use a long telephoto lens and set an exposure of around 1/1000 sec @ f/8 with an ISO of 400.

491 Shield the viewfinder eyepiece

During long-time exposures, you should shield the eyepiece to prevent stray light from affecting the AE metering and setting inappropriate exposures.

493 Lightning and fireworks

Firework displays and electrical storms are incredible photographic subjects. Manually focus the lens on infinity and set the lens aperture to around f/8. Vary the length of your exposures to change the effect. Exposures of several minutes may capture multiple lightning flashes or bursts of fireworks.

494 Star trails

Star trails make fascinating pictures and are a lot of fun to attempt. Set the camera on a tripod and set the shutter speed to Bulb (Time) setting. You will need a cable release that has a timer or can be locked in the down position. Your exposure needs to last for a minimum of 4 hours and up to 8 hours. Set an aperture of around f/8 and ISO to 200. If you are considering leaving your camera for any length of time, make sure it is secure.

Pictures for profit—shooting for stock

In this digital age, the stock photography industry is booming, and, more than ever before, amateur photographers with an eye for a picture can grab a piece of the action and make some extra cash.

495 What is stock photography?

Stock photographs are those held by picture libraries, which license images for use in advertising, publishing, and other media. If you supply pictures to libraries, in return for marketing your work the library takes a commission from each sale—usually 50 percent—although there's nothing to stop you setting up on your own and marketing direct. Shoot the right images and it can be a lucrative business; shoot the wrong ones and sales will.

496 Quality counts

Image quality is paramount if you want your images to be accepted by libraries. They must be sharp, well exposed, well composed, and commercial. If you shoot digitally, your camera must also have a minimum resolution of 10 megapixels, otherwise file sizes will be too small, and the images will be rejected.

497 Different angles

Stock photographers tend to work a subject or scene until they can't think of any other angles to capture it from. This is a good way to work, because even small variations in a composition can increase the commercial.

498 Different formats

Try supplying the same image in different formats. For example, you could make several copies of one shot then crop one to a panoramic, one to a square format, one to an upright, and so on. Although it's the same shot, by presenting it in a number of different ways it will appeal to a wider audience.

499 It's a numbers game

Stock photography is ultimately a numbers game—the more pictures you have with a library the more sales you're likely to make. However, at the same time, a small selection of top-quality pictures will sell better than a large collection of mediocre ones.

500 Compose to crop

Although tight, careful composition should be your goal, with stock photography it sometimes pays to leave a little more space around your subject than you would normally so that the image can be cropped to different shapes and formats without the meaning of the picture being lost.

501 Imagine how the picture might be used

When you're composing a photograph for sale, try to visualize how it could be used. Would there be space for text or maybe a magazine cover logo at the top? If it was used across a double-page spread, would important subject matter get lost where the pages join? Sometimes it will be necessary to shoot the same scene or subject in a variety of different ways to cover all the bases.

502 Make it suitable for different markets

The best-selling stock images are those that appeal to many different markets, so shoot accordingly. Ask yourself who might buy that picture before you take it, and if you don't know the answer, think again.

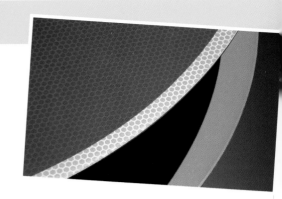

505 Be creative with composition

Stock photography used to be very traditional and quite dull, but today it's different. Buyers of stock images expect original, exciting, innovative work—as creative as if they had commissioned it themselves.

506 Mood sells

The most successful stock landscape images have mood and atmosphere. Lake scenes photographed at sunrise or sunset are classic—especially if they have soft, warm colors, calm water, reflections, and maybe a jetty and boat thrown in for good measure!

503 Model Release

Copyright and privacy laws are becoming stricter all the time, so many of the bigger global photo libraries will now reject any images that include people unless a signed model-release form is supplied. This includes travel portraits, crowd scenes, and even shots where the person or persons included aren't identifiable. But with model-release forms pictures of people will sell well.

504 Don't take pictures that date

Anything that could date a stock image will, at best, reduce its shelf life and, at worst, mean that it's rejected out of hand. So avoid traffic because license plates are date sensitive and beware of changing fashions.

Products for sale

Whether it's for auction sites or small adverts in a local paper, taking good pictures of things you want to sell will increase their sales potential tenfold.

507 Make sure they're clean

Why would anyone want to buy something that looks dirty and unloved? Exactly—so make sure everything you want to shoot is clean and tidy before reaching for a camera. It's amazing what a damp cloth and duster can achieve!

508 Choose a simple background

Potential buyers want to see the item for sale not the pattern on your dining-room wallpaper or the creases in your quilt, so always use a plain, simple background. White card is ideal for smaller objects, while a neutral-colored wall will suit bigger items.

509 Shoot different angles

Depending on what it is you're selling, it's worth shooting it from a variety of different angles so potential buyers can get the best possible idea of what they're considering spending their money on.

510 Reveal imperfections

Rather than hide imperfections, you need to show them so the eventual buyer is fully aware of the condition of the item. These imperfections should be listed in the description but also photographed in close-up.

511 Shooting in windowlight

Direct, on-camera flash is highly unflattering, so avoid it at all costs and instead use windowlight—it's much softer and easier to control. For small items place your white-card background next to a window, and you'll get far better results.

Image Editing

Postproduction

After image capture, the next stage is processing the digital file taken from the camera to make a picture with which you're totally happy. What in film-based photography historically took place in a darkroom can now be done in a well-lit room, using a computer. This process is often referred to as postproduction.

THE DIGITAL DARKROOM

At the beginning, we looked at the equipment you need to use in capturing the digital image. This part of the book considers the kit that may be needed for postproduction.

Buying a computer

There never seems to be a good time to buy a computer. As soon as you've bought one, a new, improved model becomes available, often at half the price you've just paid for yours. Here are a few hints and tips to keep you ahead of the game.

512 Processor

Most processors in new computers are perfectly capable of operating at the speed that's required for digital photography applications. Specifically, however, you should look at Windows-based PCs with the Pentium series chips, or Apple Macs with a G3 processor or higher.

513 RAM

RAM, or random access memory, is the amount of memory the computer uses to process current applications and actions. The amount of RAM your computer has is a particularly important feature for digital image processing. You should consider 256MB as a minimum and the more you have, the better the computer will perform.

514 Hard-disk drive (HDD)

The computer stores data permanently on its hard-disk drive (HDD). As digital photographs can be quite big in terms of file size—up to 60 or 70MB, or even more, it doesn't take too many of them to begin filling your HDD. Hard disk space is relatively cheap, so choose a system with a lot of it. Some 320 or 500GB is not uncommon now for a typical computer.

516 USB connections

Most systems now operate via a USB (Universal Serial Bus), which enables plug-and-play functionality. There are now two types of USB: 1 and 2. USB 2 is more modern and works at a faster speed.

517 Firewire

Another version you might hear of is FireWire (IEEE 1394), which is a high speed standard suitable for work even at professional level.

519 Laptop computers

Modern laptop computers have more than enough processing power for digital photography and the best screen technology is sufficient for professional work. They have the advantage that you can carry them with you wherever you go. However, this portability comes at a premium in terms of price. The decision between a laptop and desktop computer is ultimately a personal choice.

Laptop computers have the advantage of being portable. Courtesy of Apple.

515 Interfaces

Computer peripherals, such as scanners, graphics tablets, external disk drives, and printers, link to the computer via a cable that plugs into a socket on the computer (an interface). It's worth checking that any computer you might buy has enough of the right type of interface for your needs.

518 Desktop computers

Desktop computers tend to be less expensive than laptops, and give more computing power for your money. However, they are big and take up a fair amount of desk space. They are not portable, which means you are limited to working in one particular place.

520 Apple Mac or PC?

Again, this decision comes down to personal choice. Apple Mac computers historically were the norm in most graphics. PCs have the advantage that there is far more software written for the PC format, which may persuade you down that route if image processing isn't going to be the sole use of the machine.

Computer monitors

Another very important piece of equipment is the computer monitor. This is what you will use to review all aspects of your photographs, from sharpness to color to exposure. A quality monitor will make the job far easier and will help to ensure that what comes out of the printer is what you expected to see.

521 Screen types

There are two main types of color monitor: the CRT (cathode-ray tube) and the LCD (liquid crystal display). Each has its advantages and disadvantages.

There is more than one type of screen to choose from.

522 CRT or LCD?

CRT screens are less expensive but more bulky. They produce very high quality on-screen images, but suffer from flicker, which can make viewing for long periods of time uncomfortable. LCD screens are more expensive but have the big advantage of taking up less room on your desk and producing a stable, flicker-free image.

523 Screen size

The minimum screen size you need for image processing is 15in (38cm), and a 17in (43cm) screen or bigger is preferable.

524 Software-based calibration

Most systems now come with a software-based calibration facility built in, which are fine for general use. However, specialized third party software will provide improved accuracy and greater control over color calibration.

525 Color management

Ideally your monitor should be calibrated with your printer, so that the printer reproduces faithfully the colors you see on the screen—otherwise, you may be making unnecessary color adjustments that will show up when you print the images. You should be able to adjust the brightness and contrast on the monitor, and, ideally, to alter the shape and position of the image on screen and to control convergence.

526 Color and resolution

The screen should be capable of displaying millions of colors (which may require an upgrade to the computer's video card). Screen resolution should be a minimum of 1024 x 768 pixels; some professional monitors work at 1800 x 1440 pixels.

Scanners

So far, this book has concentrated on photographs captured by a digital camera. But you can also turn film-based pictures into digital files by scanning them. To do this you will need either a flatbed scanner or a film scanner.

527 Flatbed scanners

These have great versatility, and can be used to scan transparencies and negatives (using an adaptor), through to prints and pages from books or magazines.

528 Film scanners

Film scanners will only scan film (either transparency or negative). However, like for like, they do produce digital images of better quality.

529 Film adaptors

To scan film on a flatbed scanner you need an adaptor. If you go down the flatbed route, check that the scanner comes with an appropriate adaptor, otherwise you'll end up paying more than you thought.

530 Resolution

For good quality images that can be enlarged to a decent size (say, around 10 x 8in/ 25 x 20cm), choose a scanner that has a resolution of at least 2700ppi (points per inch).

531 Maximum density

For scanning color transparencies, if you need high-quality output, choose a model that has a maximum density of 3.6 or more. Scanners with a lower density value will lose detail in shadow and highlight areas.

532 Film formats

Different scanners will accept different sized film formats. A flatbed scanner will generally accept all formats with the right adaptor. However, some film scanners are suitable for 35mm film only.

533 Dust removal

Some scanners have a facility for digitally removing dust from the scanned file. This can be a very useful time saving function, though you should be aware that it may not be possible to remove all the scratches from a piece of film.

534 Oversampling

Some scanners use a technique known as oversampling. A built-in device samples an image more than once and averages the results. This helps to remove unwanted data (noise), which is random and therefore stripped out by sampling. The result is better image quality and reduced artifacts.

Image-editing Techniques
With digital photography, image editing is easily accomplished by computer. What follows are hints and tips for getting the most out of your digital pictures, using some of the most common and easily applied techniques. The examples are given in Photoshop Elements, a typical image-editing software program; most other editing programs will have similar tools and commands.

Cropping and resizing images

Cropping or removing unwanted parts of a picture is a skill that most digital photographers use regularly. Almost all image-editing programs have a special feature called the Crop tool for this task.

535 Using the Crop tool

Cropping is a simple matter of drawing a rectangle around the parts of the picture that you wish to keep, leaving the sections that will be removed outside of the marquee. Areas outside the cropping marquee are shaded a specific color (usually semi-transparent black) for preview purposes.

536 Fine-tune the crop

To help with fine adjustments, the edges and corners of the cropping marquee contain handles. The marquee can be resized or reshaped at any time by clicking and dragging any of the handles.

537 Customize the crop

Most image editing software shades the area of the picture that is to be removed in the crop. You can usually alter the color and opacity of this shading (called the "shield") using the settings in the Options Bar.

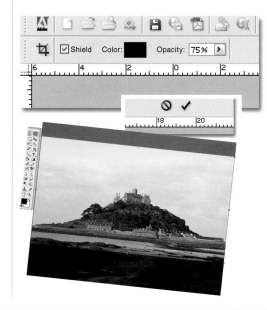

538 Set a specific size

You can make a crop of a specific size and resolution by adding these values to the Crop tool's Options Bar before drawing the marquee. Using this feature, you can crop and resize in one step. With the dimensions and resolution values set when you click and drag the Crop tool, it will only draw rectangles the size and shape of these values.

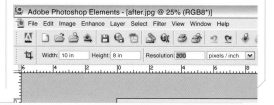

539 Prepare a photo for a particular print size

When you crop using the Size and Resolution options, Photoshop or Elements will automatically prepare the picture. In the example below, the image is to be printed on a sheet of 10 x 8in paper at a resolution of 200 pixels per inch (ppi). Cropping with these values accurately prepares the picture for print.

540 Check crop sizes

To check the size and resolution of crops, go to Image > Resize > Image Size and confirm the values in the Width, Height, and Resolution boxes.

541 Clear crop settings

The settings entered into the Width, Height, and Resolution sections of the Crop tool Options Bar remain until you click the Clear button.

542 Cropping without the Crop tool

A final on-the-fly cropping technique makes use of a drawn rectangular marquee to define the size and shape of the crop. After drawing the marquee, select the Crop command from the Image menu.

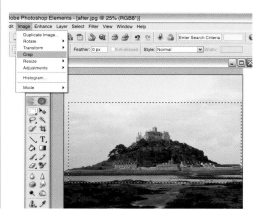

Adjusting brightness and contrast

You may find, when you come to look at an image onscreen, that it appears either too dark or too light, or even a little "flat" in tone.
To brighten or darken an image, or to make a flat image appear more vibrant and lively try using the Levels command.

543 Adjusting highlights

Open the Levels dialog box by going to Image > Adjustments > Levels.
To adjust highlights, drag the White slider (on the right) until it
corresponds with the point of the histogram where the value is
above zero. As you do, you will see the image brighten.

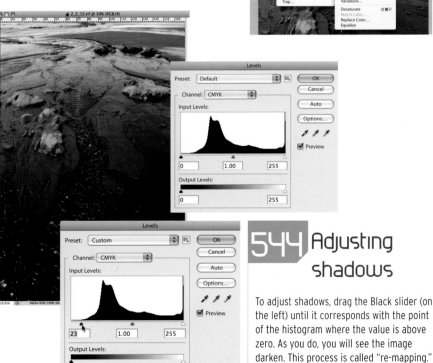

544 Adjusting shadows

To adjust shadows, drag the Black slider (on
the left) until it corresponds with the point
of the histogram where the value is above
zero. As you do, you will see the image
darken. This process is called "re-mapping."
Effectively it sets the darkest area of the
picture to black and the brightest part to
white, thereby increasing the tonal range.

545 Adjusting contrast

Levels can be used to add or remove contrast. You can alter the
level of the mid-tones in the picture without dramatically affecting
the highlights and shadows by using the Gray slider (in the middle).
This alters the overall contrast of the image.

Adjusting brightness with Curves

You can also adjust brightness and contrast levels using the Curves control. Curves is a very powerful image editing tool that could form an entire chapter of a book by itself. This is a simple introduction.

546 Select the color channel

Go to Image > Adjustments > Curves. Select the color channel you want to alter. To begin with, try leaving this at the RGB setting, which will alter all three channels together.

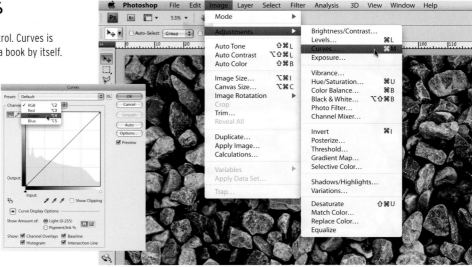

547 Adjusting the settings

Drag the cursor over the center point of the graph and shift the line up to brighten the picture and down to darken it. Keep adjusting the settings until the line's slope is sharpest where you want most of the contrast to be—shadows, mid-tones or highlights.

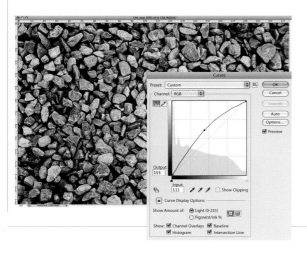

Removing dirt and dust

Dirt and dust that accumulate on the camera's sensor may appear as large, dark splodges on your pictures. These (and any similar marks, such as pimples on the skin) can be removed using the Spot Healing Brush tool.

548 Step 1

Enlarge the image (using the Zoom tool) until you can clearly see the unwanted marks. Next select the Spot Healing Brush tool. Select an appropriate size (large enough to cover the mark, if possible).

549 Step 2

Position the reference circle over the dust mark and Right click. The dust mark magically disappears.

550 Rotating an image

If the image you open is in the wrong format (e.g. a portrait shot displayed in the horizontal format), you can rotate it round to its proper setting. Go to Image > Rotate Canvas. Select an appropriate degree of rotation. For example, to change a horizontal format back to a portrait format select either 90º CCW (counterclockwise) or 90º CW (clockwise).

551 Flipping an image

Sometimes you may find that a composition works better if the image is flipped horizontally. Do this using Image > Rotate Canvas > Flip Canvas Horizontal–remembering, of course, that any words or numbers in the picture will be reversed.

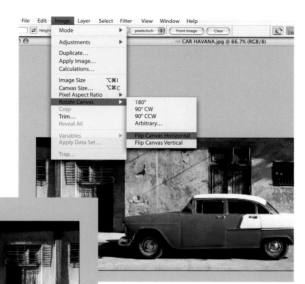

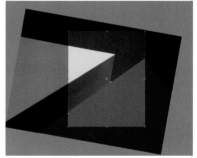

552 Straighten lopsided horizons

One of the most common compositional mistakes is not getting the horizon straight. Fortunately, this is easily remedied by selecting Image > Rotate Canvas > Arbitrary and rotating the image clockwise or counterclockwise until the horizon is straight. The image will then need to be cropped to tidy it up.

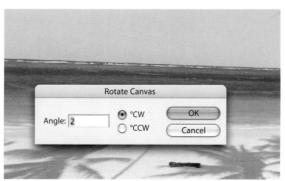

553 Tilting the image

You can use Image > Rotate Canvas > Arbitrary in a more extreme way by intentionally tilting an image to one side or the other. If necessary you can then recrop it, although this isn't essential.

Getting the colors right

Digital images are made up of three layers of color: red, green, and blue (RGB). Usually, your camera will process each image so that there is an even balance of all three colors, producing a picture that looks on the screen much as it did at the time you took it. Sometimes, however, one of the colors predominates.

554 Color Balance

Go to Image > Adjustments > Color Balance. Select Midtones and use the three sliders to adjust the color to a more appropriate tone. To adjust the color balance in the highlights and/or shadows, select the appropriate setting.

555 Variations

The Variations control (Image > Adjustments > Variations) will show you a preview of seven different images at different settings, including the current setting. This is used in assessing color balance and to preview three separate images at different brightness settings.

556 Playing with color

Some of the other controls can have an effect on how color appears in your photographs. For example, the colors in a flat scene can be made more vivid by using the Brightness/Contrast, Curves, or Levels controls.

557 Reaching saturation point

Digital images straight from the camera often lack the vibrancy of color visible in the original scene. You can easily make slightly dull pictures more colorful by adjusting the level of saturation (Image > Adjustments > Hue/Saturation) by around +15% to +20%. Be wary of oversaturating images, however, and making them look unrealistic.

Sharpening your images

If your pictures look a little soft around the edges, you can sharpen things up using the Unsharp Mask filter. While it's impossible for any software to add to information that doesn't exist in the first place (you can't make an out of focus original appear in focus), it is possible to get the most from the information that is present.

558 Sharpening options

Go to Filter > Sharpen > Unsharp Mask. Position the cursor over a portion of the picture where there is a high level of contrast. You will need to set the values for Amount (%), Radius, and Threshold (see tips 559–564).

561 Threshold

This setting sets a contrast threshold below which no sharpening takes place, and helps to keep areas of even tone, such as skies, from becoming grainy.

559 Amount

This controls the strength of the effect. Experiment with settings of between 100 and 200 until you get the right result.

560 Radius

The radius setting controls the spread of the sharpening effect. The greater the radius, the sharper the result. Watch out for unsightly halos around high contrast edges that will spoil your picture.

562 General settings

For most pictures, the following settings will give satisfactory results:
Amount (%)–Between 75 and 150%
Radius–1 or 2 pixels
Threshold–0 levels

563 Images with fine detail

For pictures where a lot of very fine detail is visible, you can increase the Amount:
Amounts (%)–Between 175 and 225%
Radius–2 pixels
Threshold–0 levels

564 Areas of tone

To improve sharpness where there is subject detail, without overstating film grain, digital noise, or other unwanted information, you can try:
Amount (%)–55%
Radius–22 pixels
Threshold–11 levels

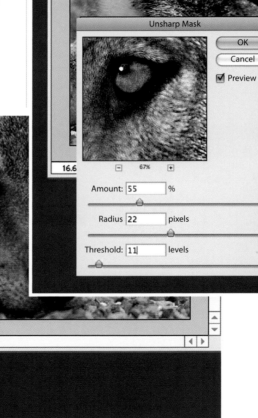

Controlling shadows and highlights

Shadows and highlights can be a challenge for any photographer. Use these simple tips to add detail and dynamism to two elements that are vital for good photography.

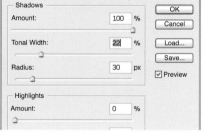

565 Lighten shadows, darken highlights

The Shadow/Highlight (Image > Adjustments > Shadow/Highlight) feature provides a great way to lighten the shadows or darken the highlights in a picture. Although similar effects could be achieved with the Curves feature, many users will find this interface easier to use.

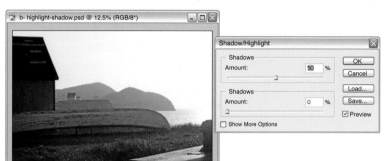

566 More shadow and highlight control

Selecting Show More Options provides more control over the changes, including extra sliders for both highlight and shadow adjustment and control of midtone contrast and color saturation. The tonal width setting adjusts the range of values that are changed by the slider. Lower values change a smaller spread of tones.

567 No more haloes with Shadow/Highlight

Use lower tonal width values in the Shadow/Highlight feature to reduce the halo effects that sometimes appear around strong dark and light edges.

Selective exposure control

Sometimes you may want to alter the exposure of just a part of a scene. For example, you may have photographed a landscape where the sky is much brighter than the foreground.

568 Select the area

Use the Magic Wand tool to select the area of the image to be adjusted. You will need to spend some time making sure that the selected area perfectly matches the horizon, as a poor selection will be very obvious. To make life a little easier, it is worth making your edits in the Quick Mask mode. To do this, press Q on the keyboard to enter Quick Mask.

569 Levels

Open the Levels dialog box and make the necessary adjustments. To turn Quick Mask off, press Q again on the keyboard.

570 Shift-select with Magic Wand

You can add any areas of the picture that the Magic Wand tool missed first time around by holding down the Shift key and Left clicking the mouse with the Magic Wand tool selected.

571 Smoothing rough edges

You can add any areas of the picture that the Magic Wand tool missed first time around by holding down the Shift key and Left clicking the mouse with the Magic Wand tool selected.

572 Select > Grow

This will expand the selection to contiguous pixels with similar colors.

573 Select > Similar

This will expand the selection to both contiguous and non-contiguous pixels with a similar color.

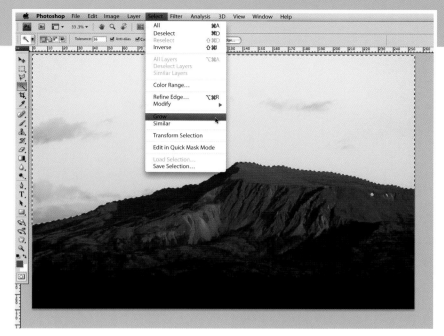

574 Select > Modify > Smooth

This will help remove the rough edges produced by Magic Wand.

Smooth Selection

Sample Radius: 1 pixels

OK
Cancel

575 Select > Modify > Expand/Contract

This will help overcome JPEG fringes around the edges of your selection.

Expand Selection

Expand By: 3 pixels

OK
Cancel

576 Select > Modify > Feather

This will select the number pixels around the selection according to the value placed in the dialog box.

577 Dodging

Another tool for controlling exposure is the Dodge tool. This acts like a brush and allows you to lighten specific areas for precise exposure control.

578 Burning

The opposite of dodging is burning the Burn tool allows you to darken areas of the picture (inset).

579 Dodging and Burning tool bar

When you select either the Dodge or Burn tools experiment with the settings in the Tool Options bar to perfect your technique.

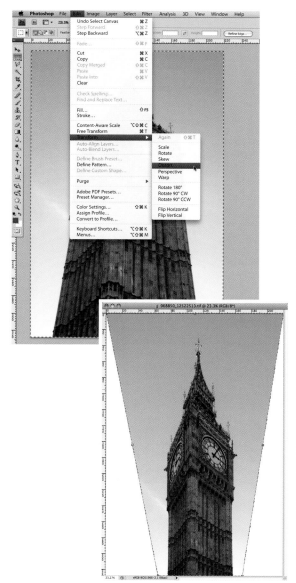

580 Deconverging verticals

One of the problems with tall buildings or monuments is that the more you angle the camera upward, the greater the distortion of the verticals. Shift lenses to overcome this are very expensive. A simpler technique is to use tools in image-editing software.

Step 1: Select the entire image and go to Edit > Transform > Distort. Drag both bottom corners inward until the sides of the building or monument look straight. Apply the changes by clicking on the √ box on the menu bar.

Step 2: Crop the new image to remove the blank canvas now visible.

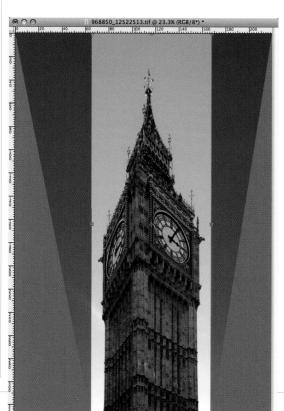

581 Using guides

Rather than using your own visual assessment as to whether the adjusted lines are vertical, you can use the guidelines in Photoshop to give an accurate measure. Go to View > New Guide and click on Vertical before entering the position of the guide. To remove the guideline(s) select View > Clear Guides.

582 Changing the sky

Don't like the existing sky in your photograph? No problem; you can change it.

Step 1: Go to Select > Color Range and click on the sky. Enlarge the image and tidy up the selection using the Magic Wand tool.

Step 2: Invert the selection using Select > Inverse. This will make the foreground the selection.

Step 3: Create a new layer by selecting Layer > New > Layer via cut.

Step 4: Open the picture containing the new sky.

Step 5: Drag the picture from the Layers dialog box onto the first image. If the new sky overlays the foreground, bring it to the back by dragging it below the foreground layer in the Layers dialog box.

583 Getting the mask right

The key to getting good results with this technique is to get the initial mask as smooth as possible. Your best bet is to zoom in using the Zoom tool and use a small Paintbrush to complete any areas missed by the initial selection tool.

584 Getting the new sky to match

It is very unlikely that the new sky will match perfectly the foreground. You can make small adjustments to the background by selecting the layer in the Layers dialog box and using Image > Adjust.

585 Realistic results

It's equally as important to make sure that the two pictures you use match. For example, a well-lit foreground would look rather odd if matched with a stormy sky.

The magic of monochrome

Black and white may be perceived as old fashioned, but to creative photographers it's the most expressive medium available.

586 Converting to black and white

Just because you take a photograph in color, it doesn't have to stay that way—converting it to mono can give it a whole new lease of life.

588 Using Channel Mixer

A more effective method of converting color to mono is using Image > Adjustments > Channel Mixer, checking the Monochrome window in the dialog box, then adjusting the sliders for the red, green, and blue channels to alter the tonal balance and contrast of the image.

587 Simple desaturation

The easiest way to convert a color image to black and white is by using Image > Adjustments > Desaturation, although serious mono workers consider this to be the least effective method, as the resulting image is often quite flat.

Using Layers

Many image-manipulation packages use the layers model as a way of extending the editing and enhancement options available to users. Being able to separate different components of a picture means that these pieces can be moved and edited independently. This is a great advantage compared to flat file editing.

Create a new layer

589 What is a layered file?

A special file type is needed if your edit features are to be maintained after a layered image is saved and reopened. In Photoshop, the PSD format supports all layer types and maintains their editability after saving and reopening. Other packages also use their own proprietary format to store their layered images. Common file formats such as JPEG and TIFF don't generally support these features. They flatten the image layers, making it impossible to edit individual image parts later.

590 Adding layers

When a picture is first downloaded from your digital camera or imported into Photoshop, it contains a single layer. By default, the program classifies the picture as a background layer. You can add extra "empty" layers to your picture by clicking the New Layer button at the bottom of the Layers palette (or top for Elements users) or choosing Layer > New > Layer. The new empty layer is positioned above your currently selected layer.

591 Automatically adding new layers

Some actions, such as adding text, automatically create a new layer for the content. This is also true when adding Adjustment and Fill layers to your image, and it occurs when selecting, copying, and pasting parts.

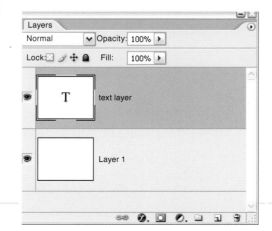

592 Viewing layers

The Layers palette in both Photoshop and Photoshop Elements displays all the layers contained in a document and their settings in the one dialog box. If this palette isn't already on screen when opening the program, choose the option from the window menu (Window > Layers).

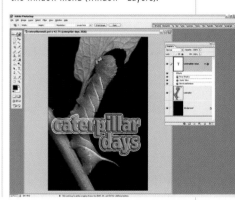

593 The layer stack

All individual layers are displayed, one on top of each other, in a "layer stack." The image is viewed from the top down through the layers. When looking at the picture onscreen, we see a preview of how the image looks when all the layers are combined. Each layer is represented by a thumbnail on the right and a name on the left.

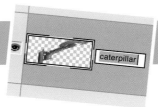

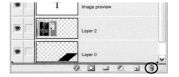

594 Name those layers!

By default, each new layer is named sequentially (layer 1, layer 2, layer 3, etc). This is fine when your image contains a few different picture parts, but for more complex illustrations it is helpful to rename the layers to match their content.

595 Editing the contents of layers

You can edit or enhance only one layer at a time. To select the layer that you want to change, you need to click on the layer. At this point, the layer will change to a different color from the rest in the stack. This layer is now the selected layer and can be edited in isolation from the others.

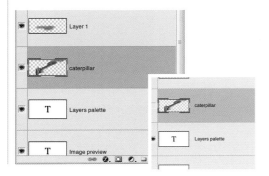

596 Hiding layers

Layers can be turned off by clicking the eye symbol on the far right of the layer so that it is no longer showing. This action removes the layer from view but not from the stack. You can turn the layer back on again by clicking the eye space.

597 Manipulating layers in the stack

Layers can be moved up and down the layer stack by clicking and dragging. Moving a layer upward will mean that its content may obscure more of the details in the layers below. Moving downward positions the layer's details further behind the parts of the layers above.

598 Layer shortcuts

• To access layers options: click sideways triangle in the upper right-hand corner of the Layers palette.
• To change the size of layer thumbnails: choose Palette Options from the Layers palette menu and select a thumbnail size.
• To make a new layer: choose Layer > New > Layer.
• To create a new Adjustment layer: choose Layer > New Adjustment Layer and then select the layer type.
• To create a new layer set: choose Layer > New > Layer Set.
• To add a style or effect to a layer: select the layer and click on the layer styles button at the bottom of the palette.

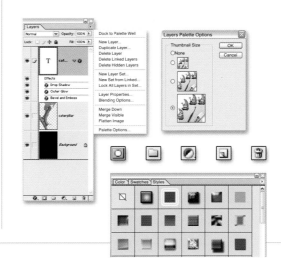

599 Moving layer contents

You can reposition the content of any layers (except background layers) using Move. Two or more layers can be linked so that when the content of one layer is moved the other details follow precisely. Click on the box on the right of the eye symbol in the layers to link together. A chain symbol indicates that the layer is linked with the selected layer.

600 Deleting layers

Unwanted layers can be deleted by dragging them to the trashcan icon at the bottom of the Layers palette. This removes the layer and its contents from the stack.

601 Layer effects

In earlier versions of Photoshop, creating a drop-shadow edge was a process that involved many steps. Thankfully, the program now includes this as a built-in effect, along with inner shadows, outer glows, inner glows, bevels and embossing, satins, plus color, gradient, and pattern overlays.

602 Adding layer effects

Add effects by clicking on the Layer Style button at the bottom of the Layers palette, or choose Layer Style from the Layer menu. The effects added are listed below the layer in the palette. You can turn effects on and off using the eye symbol and edit settings by double-clicking on them in the palette.

603 Layer opacity

As well as layer styles, or effects, the opacity of each layer can be altered by dragging the opacity slider down from 100 percent to the desired level of translucency. The lower the number, the more detail from the layers below will show through. The Opacity slider is located at the top of the Layers palette and changes the selected layer only.

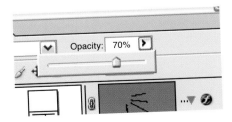

604 Layer blending modes

On the left of the opacity control is a dropdown menu containing a range of blending modes. Switching to a different blending mode alters the way in which the content of each layer interacts.

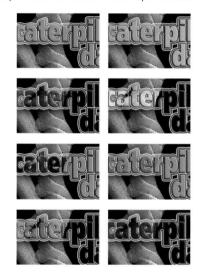

605 Layer sets

Layer sets, or Groups as they are known in Photoshop CS2 onward, are groups of layers organized into a single folder. Placing all the layers of a single picture part into a set makes these layers easier to organize.

606 Layers into sets

Layers can be moved into the set by dragging them onto the set's heading. To create a layer set, press the New Set (New Group) button at the bottom of the palette or choose Layer > New > Layer Set (Layer > New Group).

607 Layer types

• Image layers: This is the most basic and common layer type containing any picture parts or image details. An image can only have one "Background" layer.
• Text layers: These layers allow the user to edit and enhance the text after the layer has been made.
• Adjustment layers: These layers alter the layers that are arranged below them in the stack. They act as a filter through which the lower layers are viewed.

608 Enhancements

You can use Adjustment layers to perform many of the enhancement tasks that you would normally apply directly to an image layer without changing the image.

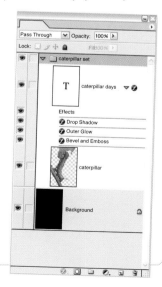

Creating panoramas

The Photomerge feature in Photoshop and Photoshop Elements create fantastic panoramic pictures by stitching together overlapping pictures to form a single image. These tips will give you a head start when producing your own panoramic vistas.

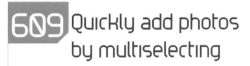

609 Quickly add photos by multiselecting

To start to stitch a series of images with Photomerge, you can multiselect the source pictures from inside the CS file browser, the Bridge application in CS2+, or the Organize Workspace in Photoshop Elements. After making the selection, you can choose Photomerge from Automate or the Photoshop Tools menu.

610 Add folders of source pictures

Alternatively, if you store your panorama source pictures in a single folder, you can add the folder contents directly in the Photomerge dialog. Start the feature and use the Browse button to locate and select the folder that contains the source pictures.

611 When automatic placement fails

When the source images are first opened into Photomerge, it will try to place them automatically. With some pictures the program will not be able to overlap them automatically. In these cases, a warning dialog will display and the pictures be placed at the top of the screen where you can organize them manually. Click and drag the pictures into the workspace, positioning them so that edge details align.

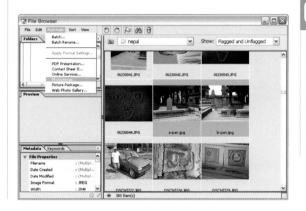

612 Get help with alignment

With the Snap to Align option checked, the program will match the edge details automatically. This helps when positioning individual images that have been selected and moved or rotated using the tools in the Toolbar.

613 The Perspective option

Using the Perspective option distorts the shape of the pictures to fit the perspective or vanishing point of a chosen image. This option can help with creating better blends between photos that have been taken with wideangle lenses. To set, select an image in the composition and then choose the Perspective option.

614 From perspective to photo shape

To remap the picture back to a rectilinear shape and ensure the best transition between successive source images, select the Cylindrical Mapping and Advanced Blending options. Click the preview button to display a predicted result. Click OK to generate the panorama as a Photoshop file.

615 Remove jagged edges in the final panorama

With the completed picture open in Photoshop, use the Crop tool to remove any jagged edges (jaggies) from the picture. This picture is now a standard Photoshop file and so can be edited and enhanced as normal.

616 Restore detail in missing areas

Often you can restore the missing detail in the border areas of a completed panorama by cloning in texture from other areas of the photograph. This is an alternative to cropping.

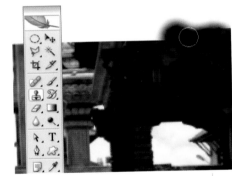

617 Keep the source pictures separate

If you want to maintain the individual images as separate layers in the final Photoshop document, click the Keep as Layers option in the Photomerge dialog before processing.

Digital toning

One of the greatest techniques of film-based printing was when a black-and-white print was transformed into something special by passing the photograph through a toning bath. In the most popular of these processes, sepia toning, the grays of the original photo were changed to subtle shades of brown. Toning was a way that photographers added "personality" to their pictures, and digital has not affected people's desire to produce pictureswith a range of toned finishes.

619 Control the toning effect

The Hue setting acts as a color selector with which you can move through the spectrum of tints. The Saturation control alters the color strength. Moving left increases the selected color's vibrancy; move to the right and eventually you end up with a grayscale picture.

621 Nondestructive toning

Wherever possible, you should apply changes to a photo via an Adjustment layer rather than directly to the picture. This way, the original picture remains intact.

618 Basic digital toning

Photoshop and Elements users should go straight to the Hue/Saturation dialog box , located in the Image > Adjust or Enhance > Adjust Color menus. Selecting Colorize places the feature in Tinting mode, which swaps grays for shades of your choice of colors.

620 Prepare a grayscale file for toning

To tone a black-and-white image, you must first provide the option for the file to store color. As most black-and-white pictures start life in the grayscale mode, the first step is to convert the photo to RGB mode via the Image > Mode > RGB Color menu item.

622 Hue/Saturation layer

With toning it is better to add a Hue/Saturation Adjustment layer by clicking on the Create Adjustment Layer icon in Layers than using Image > Adjustments > Hue/Saturation.

623 Brighten the toned picture

Don't use the Lightness slider in the Hue/Saturation dialog to make any brightness changes; instead, employ a Levels adjustment layer after the toning step is completed.

624 Toning recipes

Use this visual guide and Hue/Saturation feature settings to help predict the color of your toned prints.

625 Tinting highlights

Now let's play with the image a little more and tone the shadows and highlights different tints. This process, split toning, also finds its roots in traditional photographic printing, but unlike its counterpart, the digital equivalent is quick, predictable, and easily controllable.

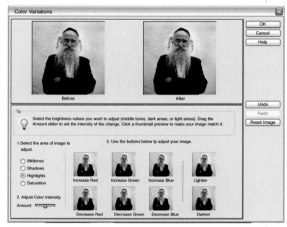

626 Split toning basics

The technique detailed here uses the Color Variations feature in Photoshop Elements (Variations in Photoshop). By selecting Highlights or Shadows in the dialog and then intentionally adding a cast to the picture by selecting a colored thumbnail, it is possible to introduce a tint to specific tonal ranges of your black-and-white photo.

627 Photoshop's Duotones

Step 1: Convert color image to grayscale. Image > Mode > Grayscale.

Step 2: Switch to Duotone mode. Image > Mode > Duotone.

Step 3: Change type from Monotone to Duotone (or Tritone or Quadtone).

Step 4: Double-click in the second ink color area to select another color.

Step 5: Double-click in the Curve area to adjust the application curve. Click OK to finish.

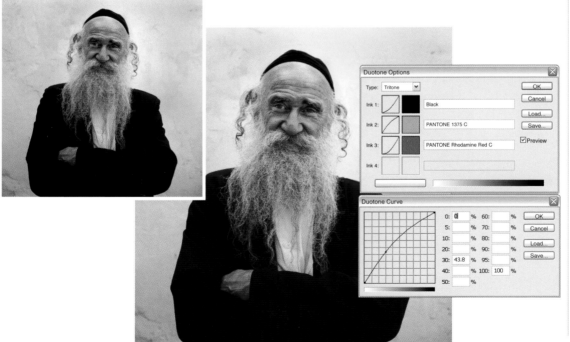

628 Beyond duotones

Tritones and quadtones extend your creative possibilities even further by adding extra inks into the equation. As you might imagine, with tritones, you mix three ink colors; with quadtones you mix four to form the tonal scale used to represent the monochrome picture.

629 Start with the simplest approach

If this all seems a little too complex, then try the Duotone presets that come bundled with Photoshop. Here, the colors and curve shapes have been designed to provide images with smooth and even transitions between tones and hues. Find these digital toning recipes in the Presets folder.

630 Adding borders

Photographs often look better framed with a border. Borders help to emphasize colors and focus attention on the image. A "framed" image will also help your pictures to stand out when posted on a Web site.

Step 1: Set the background color to the color you want the border to be.

Step 2: Go to Image > Canvas Size.

Step 3: Increase the canvas size by the depth you want for the border. For a single border around a 10 x 8in (25 x 20cm) image, plus 1in (2.5cm) is a good starting point. To add a 1in (2.5cm) border all around you'll need to increase the height and depth by 2in (5cm).

Step 4: Set the Anchor point to the center square. This will add an even-sized border all around the picture.

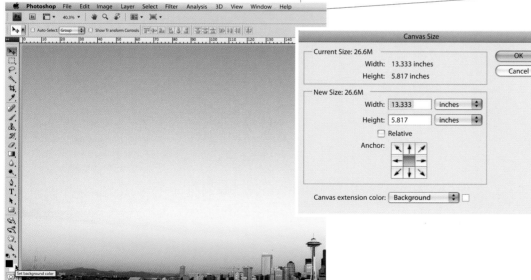

631 Multiple borders

You can add more than one border to a picture to increase the impact even more. Just follow the steps outlined above, changing the color of the second border to add contrast between the two.

Understanding channels

Channels are the way in which your image-editing program understands and manages how color is represented, which varies depending on whether your image is destined for viewing onscreen, or as a print. Learning how your software separates colors into their constituent elements opens up a whole new world of creativity...

632 What are channels?

Channels are the way in which the color in an image is represented. Most images that are created by digital cameras are made up of Red, Green, and Blue (RGB) channels. In contrast, pictures that are destined for printing are created with Cyan, Magenta, Yellow, and blacK (CMYK) to match the printing inks.

633 Viewing channels

Many image-editing programs contain features designed for managing and viewing the channels in your image. Photoshop uses a separate Channels palette (Window > Channels). This breaks the full color picture into its various color parts.

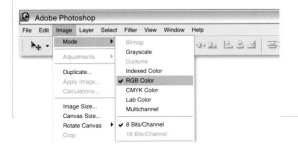

634 Channels and file size

Changing the number of channels also affects the file size of a picture. Four-channel CMYK images are bigger than three-channel RGB pictures, which are roughly three times larger than single-channel grayscale images.

635 Changing color mode

Though most editing and enhancement work can be performed on the RGB file, the digital photographer may sometimes need to change color modes. There is a range of conversion options located under the Mode menu (Image > Mode) in Photoshop.

636 Should you change channels for print?

For most image-editing and enhancement tasks, RGB color mode is all you will ever need. A question often asked by photographers is "Given that my ink-jet printer uses CMYK inks, should I change my photograph to CMYK before printing?" Logic says yes, but practically speaking this type of conversion is best handled by your printer's driver software. Most modern desktop printers are optimized for RGB output even if their ink set is CMYK.

637 Color modes and channel options

• RGB: Consisting of Red, Green, and Blue channels, most digital camera and scanner output is in this mode.
• CMYK: Designed to replicate the ink sets used to print magazines, newspapers, and books, this mode is made from Cyan, Magenta, Yellow, and Black channels.
• LAB: Consisting of Lightness, A color (green-red), and B color (blue-yellow), this mode is used by professionals when they want to enhance details without altering color. By selecting the L channel and then performing their changes, only the image details are affected.
• Grayscale: Consisting of a single black channel, this mode is used for monochrome pictures.

High-bit files

Many different types of photographic hardware can capture "high bit" image files. As resolution and channel management prepares to take another giant leap ahead in terms of quality, then you need to get to grips with how it all works. So here are some tips for understanding and managing high-bit files.

638 High resolution is not the only factor

Most of us are very aware of the impact that resolution has on the quality of our images. But high resolution is only half the image quality story. The number of colors in an image is also a factor that contributes to the overall quality of the photograph.

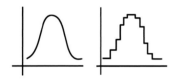

639 Beyond 8 bits per channel

Many modern cameras and scanners are now capable of capturing 16 bits per channel; this is known as "high bit" capture. This means that each of the three colors can have 65,536 different levels and the image 281,474,976 million colors. More colors equals better quality.

640 The more colors, the better

Capturing images in High-bit mode provides a larger number of colors for your camera or scanner to construct your image with. This in turn leads to better color and tone in the digital version of the continuous-tone original.

641 High beats low

Global editing and enhancement changes made to a high-bit file will always yield a better quality result than when the same changes are applied to a low-bit image.

642 No poster pin-ups

Major enhancement of the shadow and highlight areas in a high-bit image are less likely to produce posterized tones than they would in a low-bit version.

643 A new level of image

More subtle changes and variations are possible when adjusting the tones of a high-bit photograph using Levels or Curves than is possible with low-bit images.

644 All about bits...

Each digital file you create (capture or scan) is capable of representing a specific number of colors. This capability, usually referred to as the "mode" or "color depth" of the picture, is expressed in terms of the number of "bits."

645 Multimillion hues

Most images these days are created in 24-bit mode (8 bits per color channel). This means that each of the three-color channels (red, green, and blue) is capable of displaying 256 levels of color (or 8 bits) each. When the channels are combined, a 24-bit image can contain 16.7 million hues.

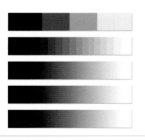

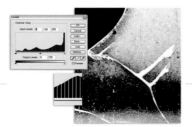

Adding artistry

Image editing isn't always about improving the photographic quality of your pictures. Sometimes you may want to experiment with the more artistic side of the process.

Artistic interpretations

Most image-editing software allows you to create different artistic interpretations of your photographs using filters. Here we'll look at some of those available to Photoshop and Photoshop Elements. It's just a small selection and you can download many more from the Internet. Each style can be accessed from the Filter menu. Experiment with the various value settings, and review the outcome in the preview box before committing to the change.

646 Film grain

Filter > Artistic > Film Grain

This can add an evocative touch particularly to black and white pictures.

647 Noise

Filter > Noise > Add Noise

Like film grain, noise can be used to make an artistic statement. Be careful not to overdo this effect.

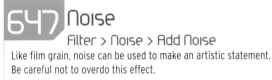

648 Motion blur

Filter > Blur > Motion Blur

This can give wildlife and sporting pictures a sense
of energy. Be sure to use a picture where the
subject was moving.

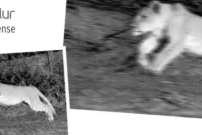

649 Radial blur

Filter > blur > Radial blur

This one is a little more arty. It needs to be used with care,
so as not to look too manufactured

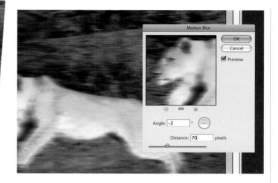

650 Spherize

Filter > Distort > Spherize

Here's a neat little trick to achieve a fisheye lens effect.

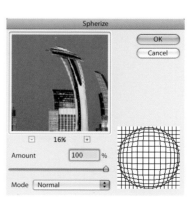

Lighting effects

It's not always possible to achieve the lighting effects you want, either in the field or in the studio. Help is at hand with Photoshop Lighting Effects. Some of the more useful options are illustrated here. With each, it's worth playing with the controls to discover all the variations you can achieve.

651 Flood Light

To achieve a flood light effect, go to Filter > Render > Lighting Effects and Flood Light under the Style menu.

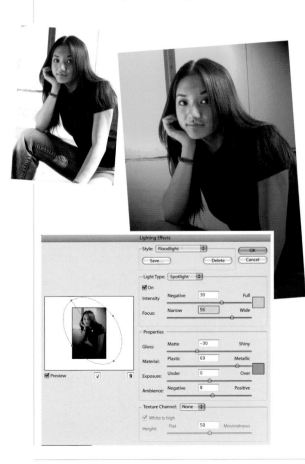

652 Flashlight

To achieve a flashlight effect, go to Filter > Render > Lighting Effects and Flashlight under the Style menu.

653 Soft Omni

To achieve a soft omni light effect, go to Filter > Render > Lighting Effects and Soft Omni under the Style menu.

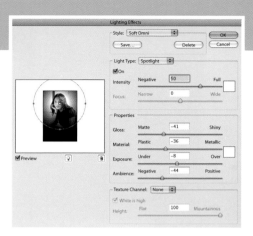

654 Soft Spotlight

To achieve a soft spotlight effect, go to Filter > Render > Lighting Effects and Soft Spotlight under the Style menu.

655 Blue Omni

To achieve a flood light effect, go to Filter > Render > Lighting Effects and Blue Omni under the Style menu.

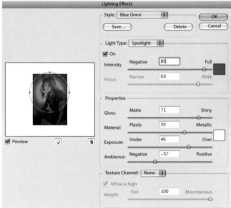

Creative art finishes

Your picture is a photograph, but it doesn't have to stay that way. You can use the Filter menu to give your images an artistic finish. As with most of these tools, it's worth experimenting. The following are filters that work well with most subjects.

656 Watercolor
Filter > Artistic >
Watercolor

658 Colored Pencil
Filter > Artistic >
Colored Pencil

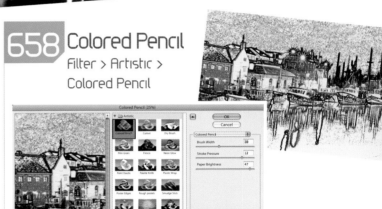

657 Rough Pastels
Filter > Artistic >
Rough Pastels

659 Mosaic Tiles
Filter > Texture >
Mosaic Tiles

660 Adding text

When you create posters, calendars, postcards, or greetings cards you will probably also want to add some text to the picture.

Step 1: Decide where on your photograph you want the text to appear and what you want the message to say.

Step 2: Click on the Text tool.

Step 3: Choose a style (font), size, and color of text from the menu bar at the top of the screen.

Step 4: Position the cursor over the center of the picture (you can move the text to its exact position later) and type out your chosen message.

Step 5: Once you're happy with the wording, style, color, and size, click on the Move tool and position the text. You can also use this tool to enlarge or rotate the text.

661 Altering text

Once you have written the text and saved the file you can edit at a later date by clicking on the Text tool and highlighting the text with the cursor.

General tips on using Photoshop

If you use Photoshop or Photoshop Elements then you already have a packed instruction manual to plough through, but here are some simple and accessible hints and tips for a stress-free working life with your image-editing software...

662 Calibrate your screen

Calibrating your screen is the start of obtaining predictable results. Before starting to perform critical tonal or color corrections to your images, you need to use a feature like the Adobe Gamma screen calibration program to optimize your display settings. This utility profiles your screen so that colors and tones display accurately (and consistently with other monitors).

663 Undo unwanted editing changes

If you want to undo an edit, use the Ctrl (or Apple) Z keyboard shortcut to undo your last action, and use Ctrl + Alt + Z to undo multiple steps sequentially.

664 Hassle-free even borders

Instead of working out exactly how much the new dimensions of a picture will be with a border added, try ticking the Relative button in the Canvas Size dialog (Image > Canvas Size) and then input the size of the extra width and height you want to add to the picture.

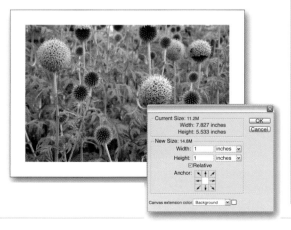

665 Adapt the Healing brush

You can make the Healing brush behave more like the Clone (Rubber Stamp) tool by switching the Healing brush's blending mode to Replace. In this mode, the sampled area is not blended with the pixels below but pasted over them.

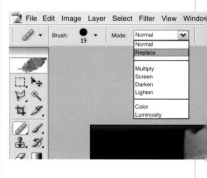

666 Preview filter changes at 100 percent

When applying filters, always make sure that your image (or preview thumbnail) is displaying at 100 percent or greater so that you can check the results more closely before hitting OK.

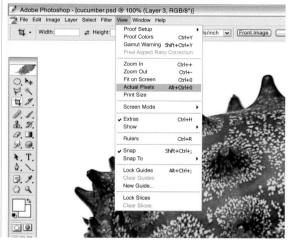

668 Master selection techniques

Often it is the quality of the selections used in editing and enhancing techniques that determines how professional the results look. Practice the many selecting techniques available in Photoshop to improve your skills.

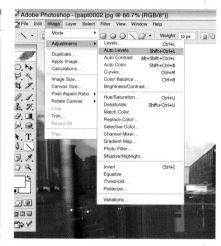

667 View Actual Pixels when sharpening

When sharpening an image using the Unsharp Mask, always view the results at Actual Pixels (View > Actual Pixels) as then you'll see an accurate interpretation of the sharpening effect.

669 Learn keyboard shortcuts

Take note and memorize the keyboard shortcuts of your most-used menu selections or tools. Using them will speed up your editing work. This utility profiles your screen so that colors and tones display accurately (and consistently with other monitors).

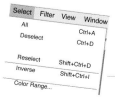

670 Use Auto features sparingly

Auto features are quick but lack the control of the manual versions. For best results, use an editing or enhancement method that allows you to make manual adjustments.

671 Control filter effects

You can fade filters immediately after applying by selecting Edit > Fade. Alternatively, try applying the filter to a copy of the picture layer and then using the opacity slider to blend the layer with the original.

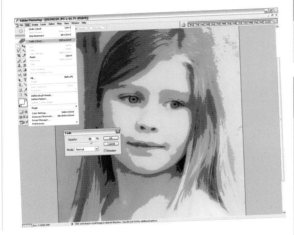

672 Move selections

Move a selection (the moving dotted line) using the arrow keys on the keyboard. Hitting a key will nudge the selection along by one pixel. Alternatively, with the Marquee tool still active, click and drag inside the selection.

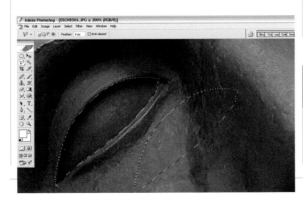

673 Quick document info

Right-clicking on the title bar of your image displays a popup menu containing: Duplicate, Image Size, Canvas Size, File Info, and Page Setup.

674 Select any hard-to-see edges

When the edge of a dark object gets lost in the background, copy the image layer, adjusting its brightness until the edge is visible, and then use this layer to create the selection. Trash the copied layer and use the selection on the original.

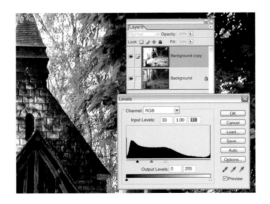

675 Roll up your palettes!

Keep your desktop clutter-free by rolling up palettes until you need them. Double-click the top bar of the palette to roll up and unroll.

676 Free up memory

Free up space to execute complex corrections on big images by purging Photoshop's memory (Edit > Purge). You can free up all the memory using Purge > All, or just those sections filled with Clipboard (Purge > Clipboard), History (Purge > History), or Undo (Purge > Undo) components.

677 Save original files uncompressed

Use the native file format in Photoshop (.psd) to save your original files. This will ensure that the best quality and features of your images are maintained.

678 Move multiple layers together

To move a number of objects that occupy different layers, select one of the image layers and then click the space next to the eye icon of each other layer. A chain icon appears to show that the layers are now linked. Once linked, the objects can be moved or adjusted using any of the transformation tools.

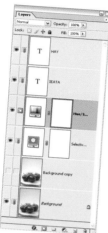

679 Convert background layer to image layer

To convert a background layer to an image layer, double-click on the layer's label and add a title. It can now be edited like any other layer.

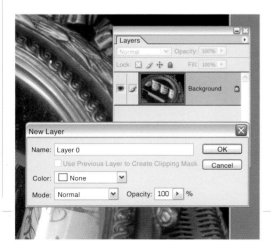

680 Snap off

By default, Photoshop will usually snap the edge marquees and cropping selections to the edge of the document. To regain control over your selection near the document edges, hold down the Ctrl (or Apple) key after you click and drag. To turn off Snap, go to View > Snap.

681 Move the view while in action

Change to the Hand tool (to move your image) by holding down the spacebar. Use the spacebar then click and drag to move a picture no matter what your current tool selection is. Releasing the spacebar returns Photoshop to the previous tool (except when using the Text tool).

682 Shift things into proportion

Keep object height and width in proportion by holding down the Shift key while moving one of the corner handles. Use the Shift key in conjunction with drawing and marquee tools to draw perfect squares or circles.

683 Quick fills

Fill a layer with the foreground color by clicking Alt + Backspace. To fill with the background color instead, use Ctrl + Backspace.

684 Non-destructive changes

Use Photoshop's Adjustment layers to make changes to your images. Then, if need be, these adjustments can be further refined, or removed altogether, with no detrimental effects left on the original picture.

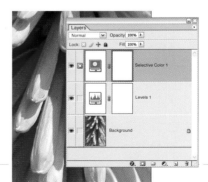

685 Add a colored border

Use the Select > All command and then stroke the selection (Edit > Stroke) with settings of your choice of pixel width and color on the inside of the selection. Click the color swatch to change the color of the border.

686 Create outlined text

With the Text layer selected, choose Layer > Layer Style > Stroke. Alter the size, position, and color of the outline (or stroke) in the Stroke dialog.

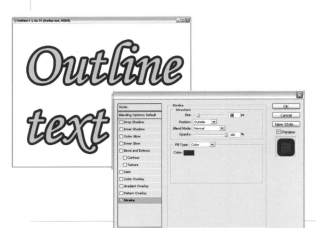

687 Hide all the palettes

Once you have selected a tool, you can hide all the palettes and dialogs by hitting the Tab key. Using Shift + Tab keeps the toolbar visible.

688 Dock unused palettes

Clear your workspace by dragging unused palettes that you want to access later to the dock. Each palette is then accessed by clicking on the appropriate tab at the top of the box.

689 Zoom in to ensure accuracy

If you have a small screen, it is still possible to work on fine detail within an image by zooming in to the precise area that you wish to work on. Zoom in is Ctrl + and out Ctrl -.

690 Change screen mode

Change from standard to full-screen mode with menu bar by clicking the F key. Change to the full-screen mode with no menu bar and a black background by clicking F again.

691 Learn quick opacity changes

To change the opacity of the currently active tool, use the number keys on your keyboard. Pressing 1 will give you 10 percent; 3 gives you 30 percent; 23 gives you 23 percent; and 0 gives you 100 percent.

692 Numbers on the go

Change the number settings for type sizes, adjustment percentages, scaling, and so on by using the up and down arrow keys. Using Shift with the arrow keys makes changes of larger values.

693 Hide selections and guides

The keystrokes Ctrl + H can be used to hide selection edges, text highlighting, slices for the Web, and guides. Be sure to remember that these objects are still there!

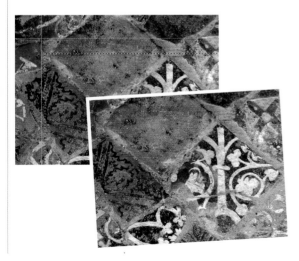

694 Remove fringes

Copy and paste an object from a light background onto a dark background and you often see a white outline. To remove this fringe, choose Layer > Matting > Defringe and use a setting of 1. The same applies for dark onto light.

695 Instant digital polarizing filter

Make a selection of the blue section of the image and then choose Layer > New Fill Layer > Solid Color. Set the mode to Color Burn and then click OK. Choose a shade of gray from the color picker that pops up. The darker the gray, the stronger the polarizing effect.

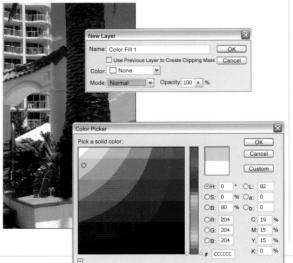

696 Copy all layers in a selection

Holding the Shift key down while copying a selection (Ctrl + C) will copy all the layers in the selection. Alternatively, you can create the same result by making the selection and then choosing Edit > Copy Merged.

697 Make exact fits

Holding down the Shift key while dragging selections or layers between images of the same dimensions will keep the transferred components in exactly the same position. If the documents are different sizes, using the Shift key will mean that the copied component will be placed in the center of the new document.

698 Watch out for slicing

If a "01" appears in the upper left corner of your open Photoshop documents, then you have clicked on the Slice tool (perhaps accidentally). To hide the slices display select View > Show > Slices.

699 Mac translator for keystrokes

Windows	Shift	Alt	Ctrl
Macintosh	Shift	Option	Apple

700 Multiple filters

You can apply the last-used filter again to your image by clicking Ctrl + F. This shortcut uses the same settings that were applied the first time. To bring up the dialog to allow a change of settings, hold down the Alt key as well as Ctrl + F.

701 Automate your most used techniques

Use the Photoshop Actions feature to record the various steps in your favorite technique. When you next want to create this effect, simply open the image and play back the action from the Actions palette.

702 Pictures within a picture

If you take a close look at one of your favorite photographs, chances are you'll find a number of other more selective compositions within the overall scene. These can be isolated by cropping and copying to create scenes within a scene.

703 Adding a keyline

A narrow black line around the edge of an image can also look highly effective. To create one, open the image then go to Select > All then Edit > Stroke, enter a small value such as 3 or 5 in the Width window, click OK, and a fine black keyline will be created. Next, increase the canvas size a little to show the keyline off.

704 Creative borders

Instead of a keyline, try experimenting with bolder borders. To create the basic border, increase the canvas size by 10 or 15 percent and use black as the extension color. All you do then is paint away the outer edges of the border using the Eraser tool and the Pastel Medium Tip brush found in the Dry Media Brushes palette.

705 Increase the canvas size

It's easier to assess an image on a monitor screen if it's set against a plain background. Create one simply by increasing the canvas size of the image and using either white or black as the canvas color—Image > Canvas Size.

Output

Making the most of your work
Whatever kind of pictures you take, there is a wide range of options when it comes to using them. Over the next few pages we'll take a look out how to make the most of your images once you've completed post-production editing.

Printing and printers

There are several different printer technologies that can turn your digital pictures into photographs. The most popular, at the moment, is the ink-jet printer, followed by dye sublimation and laser machines. Here are some tips to help you understand the printing process and get to grips with some of the techniques and options.

706 Creating millions of colors

Get to know a bit about printing, as it will help you make better pictures. Most commercial print systems (such as those used by magazines and newspapers) use a color separation technique known as CMYK (Cyan, Magenta, Yellow, and Black). The printer lays down a series of tiny dots of these colors. Looking at the picture from a distance, creates the illusion of many colors. This is different to the system used by your computer monitor, which is based on just three colors—Red, Green, and Blue (RGB mode).

707 Creating tone with dots

To create darker and lighter colors, the printer produces colored dots at varying sizes. The lighter tones are created by printing small dots so that more of the white paper base shows through. The darker tones in the image are made with larger dots leaving less paper showing. This system is called halftoning. In traditional printing, different dot sizes, and therefore tone, are created by screening the photograph. In desktop digital printing, different shades are created using simulated halftones.

708 Ink-jet printers

Ink-jet printers provide the cheapest way of entering the world of desktop printing. Their ability to produce great photographs are based on a combination of fine detail and seamless graduation of color and tone. The machines contain a series of cartridges filled with liquid ink, which is forced through a set of tiny print nozzles using either heat or pressure as the printing head moves back and forth across the paper. It's worth doing research before you buy, and finding out how expensive the print cartridges are and whether they have to be replaced quickly. It may be more cost-effective to buy a slightly more expensive printer that works efficiently and cheaply than to go for a bargain. Shop around and ask questions!

709 Dye sublimation printers

If you're serious about photography, it might be worth exploring dye sublimation printers, which create prints by using a heating element to transfer a series of overlapping transparent dyes onto a specially treated paper. This gives the image a "continuous tone" look at relatively low resolutions (300dpi) compared to ink-jets.

710 Laser printers

If you run a small or home business, have a look at laser printers. More and more are capable of producing acceptable color output. Laser printers are expensive to buy but very inexpensive to run, and for businesses that regularly produce short runs of color brochures, a color laser may be a cost-effective alternative to commercial printing. However, toner supplies might be harder to source than ink-jet cartridges, and laser printers are too expensive for light use.

711 Dye-based inks

Most standard cartridges found in entry-level and moderately priced printers use dye-based inks. They are generally easy to use and have fewer problems with streaking, long drying times, and puddling than pigmented inks. Most dye-based ink sets are capable of a greater range of more vibrant colors than their pigment-based equivalents. The downside is that dye-based sets have a shorter lifespan than pigmented options.

712 Pigment-based inks

These products generally have a longer predicted archival life than most dye-based inks and are also more water- and humidity-resistant. They are generally available for use in high-end professional and semi-professional printers. But be warned: these ink sets can be more difficult to use and some brands do not have the same vibrancy, color, or density range as their dye-based equivalents.

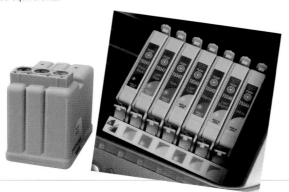

713 Specialist monochrome ink sets

Some ink sets contain several different gray inks as well as black and are designed for dedicated black-and-white enthusiasts. The inks are used to print monochrome prints that are more neutral than those traditionally output from jet printers using CMYK. Such ink sets are found in photographic printers with seven or more inks.

714 Six inks or four?

Most ink-jet printers use four ink colors (yellow, magenta, cyan, and black). Newer and–usually–more expensive models also have two extra ink colors: photo-cyan and photo-magenta. Another model has a seventh ink color, gray. All other things being equal, the more ink colors you have, the better the quality of the final output.

715 Ink cartridges

Some printers keep all the color inks in an integrated cartridge (the black ink is always separate), while others have separate cartridges for each different color. With an integrated cartridge you will have to replace the whole cartridge once any one of the ink colors runs out, whether or not the other ink colors are spent. Here, your choice has little to do with image quality and more to do with economy in use.

Paper types

Your paper choice affects the look of the print. For best results, and to minimize printer failure, use paper that is designed to work with your type of printer.

716 Paper

Computer stores offer a huge variety of printing paper, from fine art to high gloss and from postcard to poster size, panoramic, and preformed greetings cards. Which you buy is largely down to personal choice and it's worth testing paper out on a small scale first. It might be tempting to go for paper made by the same company as your printer, but non-proprietary brands often produce better quality images.

717 Paper size and quality

The thickness of the paper and its coating will partly determine print quality. For photo-quality images, use a thicker paper (around 270gsm) with a gloss finish. For more artistic reproductions and special effects, try out some of the art papers available, such as watercolor, hessian, and canvas finishes.

718 Coated papers

The coating is a special ink-receptive layer that increases the paper's ability to produce sharp photorealistic results with a wide color gamut and a rich maximum black (high D-max). Most ink-jet papers fall into this category.

719 Uncoated papers

Uncoated papers can still be used with most printing equipment, but changes in the printing setup may be necessary to get good results. Generally, standard office or copy paper as well as traditional watercolor and fine art papers fall into this category. Most photographers don't use uncoated papers because the ink soaks into the paper, producing fuzzier images.

720 Swellable papers

These papers are the most sophisticated of all ink-jet papers. As part of the printing process, a gelatin-like coating on the paper swells to encapsulate the ink. This creates an image that is much more resistant to fading than if the same image were printed on a standard coated or uncoated paper.

Making prints

Making a print from your digital file is likely to be one of the first and most frequent things you want to do.

Making sure that the print you get looks like the picture you created on the computer screen, however, isn't always as easy as it sounds. Here are some tips for making sure that you get what you want.

Image resolution

Mentioned briefly earlier, let's revisit this often confusing area with specific reference to printing. The true dimensions of any digital file are measured in pixels, not inches or centimeters. These dimensions indicate the total number of samples of the scene (or negative/print when scanned) that were made to form the file. It is only when an image's resolution is chosen that these dimensions will be translated into a print size measured in inches or centimeters.

721 What is image resolution?

It determines how the digital information is spread over the print surface. If a setting of 100dpi is chosen, the print will use 100 pixels for each inch that is printed. If the image is 3000 pixels wide then this will result in a print that is 30in wide. If the image resolution is set to 300 dpi, the resultant print will only be 10in wide, as three times as many pixels are used for every inch of the print. The same digital file can have many different printed sizes.

723 Printer resolution

Printer resolution refers to the number of ink droplets placed on the page per inch of paper. Most modern printers are capable of 3,000 dots per inch. This value does not relate to the image resolution. It is a measure of the machine's performance, not the spread of pixels.

722 Changing image resolution

The resolution of the image can be changed using features like Photoshop's Image Size command (Image > Image Size). This dialog contains options for changing the overall number of pixels as well as the resolution in a picture. To ensure that you adjust only the resolution value, deselect the resample image option first and then input a new setting into the resolution section of the document size area.

724 Changing printing resolution

The resolution that your printer uses is controlled via the printer driver. In this example, the setting is described as print quality and is only available once the advanced printer settings are selected.

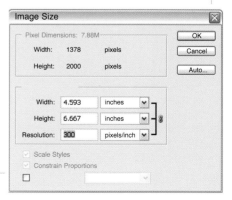

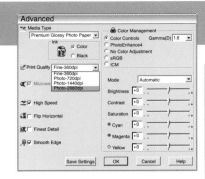

725 Hidden print resolution control

With some printers, print resolution cannot be changed specifically and no control or menu is included for this purpose. But as print resolution is linked with the type of media or paper you print on, selecting a better quality surface will result in a better print.

726 Optimum printing resolution

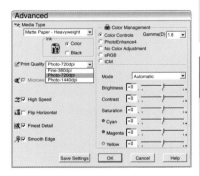

Keep in mind that different printing technologies have different optimum resolutions. For example, perfectly acceptable photographic images are produced on dye sublimation machines with a printing resolution as low as 300dpi. The same appearance of photographic quality may require a setting of 1440dpi on an ink-jet machine.

727 Optimal image resolutions for print

The modern ink-jet printer is capable of amazingly fine detail. A typical photographic-quality Epson printer is able to print at 5760dpi when set on its finest settings. Logic dictates that if you were to make the best-quality print from this machine then you need to make sure image resolution matched this print resolution. This may be logical but it isn't practical, and the solution is to determine your printer's optimum resolution for printing. Test your printer by outputting a variety of pictures with image resolutions ranging from 100dpi to 800dpi.

Make sure that all photos are made with the machine set on its best quality setting (5760dpi). The results will show that major changes in print quality are noticeable to the naked eye with resolutions up to about 300dpi. Settings higher than this result in very little change. Armed with this information, getting the best from your printer is just a matter of setting its resolution to the finest possible and adjusting your images to the optimal image resolution, which is generally between 200 and 300ppi.

728 Printer properties using automatic settings

The printer properties dialog box contains an array of settings and controls that act as the last fine-tuning step in outputting your digital image. Most new users follow the "automatic everything" approach to help limit the chances of things going wrong. For most scenarios, this type of approach produces good-quality results, but if you want a little more control you will have to abandon the "auto" route.

729 Print controls versus software controls

To help resolve the confusion that often surrounds making adjustments to your printed output, it is useful to separate the controls into two sections: those adjusted by the software program such as Photoshop, and those that control the hardware or printer itself. Each section plays an important role. The editing program controls remain the same irrespective of the printer you are outputting to, whereas the hardware dialogs change according to the printer you are using.

730 Manual printer control

When working manually, there are several adjustments that can be made via the printer control dialog:
• the paper size, orientation, and surface type
• the dots per inch that the printer will place onto the page (printer resolution), and
• color and tone control.

Although using automatic settings provides a less confusing approach to printing, making manual adjustments to the printer setup provides you with more creative possibilities.

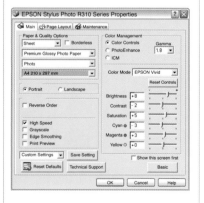

731 Producing a contact sheet

You can produce a contact sheet of images in Photoshop and most other image-editing software. This is a useful way to share a lot of pictures with friends and family without having to print them off individually.

Step 1: Go to File > Automate > Contact Sheet.

Step 2: Choose your source file from the Browse menu.

Step 3: Next enter the document dimensions and the print resolution.

Step 4: Enter the number of images to appear on each page (the more images, the smaller they will be printed).

Step 5: Select the Use File Name as Caption box if you want the file name to be printed under each photograph.

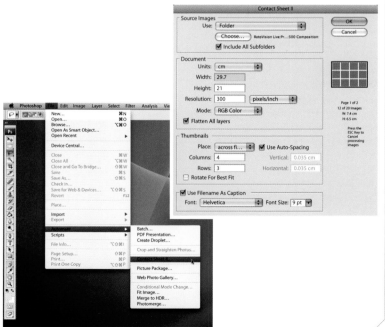

732 Creating a panorama

It's easy to create a panorama from a series of individual shots using Photoshop's Photomerge functionality.

Step 1: Either shoot or source a series of images that overlap slightly at each edge. If you're careful you can do this with just a handheld camera, but it's easier if you use a tripod to swivel the camera from left to right.

Step 2: Go to File > Automate > Photomerge and add each of the images you want to include in your panorama to the list by either browsing for the files, or by first opening the images and using the Add Open Files option. Select the Auto option for the layout for a basic panoramic image without added perspective or distortion.

Step 3: All added images will be automatically aligned to form one large panoramic shot. Some cropping may be required to remove misaligned elements of the image at the edges.

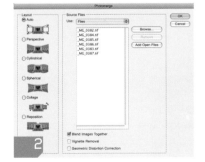

Online galleries

Uploading your photographs to the Internet is now a lot easier than it used to be and you no longer need to operate your own website to do it. A plethora of online photo galleries have opened up on the Internet, many offering a host of different services. Here are a few names to check out. Most are free to join and by following the onscreen instructions, it's simple to upload your images.

733 Flickr

www.flickr.com

734 Photobucket

www.photobucket.com

735 Fotki

www.fotki.com

736 Smugmug

www.smugmug.com

737 PhotoIsland

www.photoisland.com

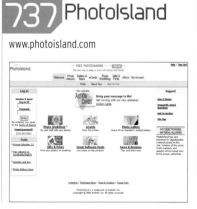

738 Shutterfly

www.shutterfly.com

739 Kodak Gallery

www.kodakgallery.com

Camera care

Your camera is an expensive bit of kit, full of delicate precision engineering, so it's worth looking after it. The build and durability of different cameras varies, depending on their specification. High-end professional-specification cameras are often designed to withstand heavy use in camera-hostile environments. They have metal body frames, durable coverings, and openings sealed to prevent penetration by dirt, dust, and moisture. At the opposite end of the scale, cameras may be designed only for light use, and certainly not in extreme environments.

740 Use your camera wisely

Use your camera as it was intended. If you are considering a trip to the Antarctic, or into a rainforest, check to see whether your camera is built for it. If it isn't, get suitable protection, such as a rain cover.

741 Avoid heavy knocks

Cameras today are computers, with all the intricate electronics that you would associate with your desktop PC or laptop. They need to be treated with care and, while most cameras will survive a slight knock or bump, they should be protected from harder impact.

742 Lens care

You should be particularly careful when cleaning the lens. Use a blower brush to remove any large particles of dust and a special microfiber lens cloth to wipe away any surface marks. When using the lens cloth, clean in a circular motion from the center outward.

743 Changing lenses

If you're using a DSLR, always turn off the camera when changing lenses to avoid excessive dust attaching to the sensor. Whenever possible, change lenses using a plastic bag to isolate the camera from the environment.

744 Filters

You obviously need to take as much care in cleaning any filters you use as in cleaning the lens. Use the same techniques described in Tip 743.

745 Dust and dirt

Dust and dirt have a habit of getting into every little nook and cranny on a camera and finally they can work their way onto the tiny microchips inside. Using an air spray is the best way to keep the camera clean. Every so often, and particularly if you've been on the beach or in a dusty environment, give the camera body a good going over with an air spray, but avoid the front element of the lens.

746 Cleaning the photo-sensor

The sensor in DSLR cameras attract dust, which then materializes as specks and blotches on your digital pictures. There is little you can do about this—it's just one of those things, and all camera manufacturers advise that you take the camera to an authorized service center for cleaning. Unfortunately, the cost of this, if you use your camera regularly, soon adds up. It's not advisable to clean your own photo-sensor—they are very delicate and sensitive bits of technology and it's easy for them to be damaged beyond repair. However, if you decide to give it a go at your own risk, here are some suggestions.

Step 1: Make a purpose-made swab (such as those made by Photographic Solutions Inc.) and apply just two drops of optical cleaning fluid (supplied by the same company).

Step 2: Remove the camera lens or body cap and flip the mirror to the up position, following the instructions in your camera's instruction manual.

Step 3: With the mirror in the up position gently wipe the swab across the sensor, in one motion and in one direction only. Then, turn the swab over and repeat the process in the opposite direction.

Step 4: Remove the swab and return the mirror back to its normal position. Then replace the camera lens or body cap.

747 Storage

When storing the camera at home, always attach the caps to the camera body and lenses, if stored separately, and keep the camera in a cool, dry place.

748 Remove batteries

Remove batteries from the camera whenever you are storing it for long periods.

749 Firmware upgrades

Most manufacturers provide upgrades to their DSLR cameras, in much the same way that software manufacturers provide updates to software packages without releasing a completely new version. These upgrades are known as firmware upgrades, and are released periodically, usually via the Internet. Watch for news on firmware upgrades on websites such as www.dpreview.com, as well as the manufacturer's own sites.

Digital Video

Reasons for videomaking
Whether it's the most typical of family occasions, or the chance to capture a once-in-a-lifetime moment, there is always an impulse that makes us hit the record button on a camcorder.

In this section you'll find tips on equipment and techniques, accessories and editing, and showing your video footage.

What's on a camcorder?
There is a wide variety of features that you'll find on virtually every camcorder. Here are some of the key functions, and what you might use them for.

750 On automatic
You can use Automatic controls to make shooting your video easier. The camcorder will take care of major controls such as Focus and Exposure to make sure your video looks as good as possible. This is especially useful if you haven't got time to switch on and set any Manual controls.

751 Manual labor
Use Manual controls when you can, as you can make amendments and corrections to your video as you go, so that the scene is sharp and the color levels look right. Using Manual controls takes longer to master, but they give you more creative control.

752 Zoom control
The Zoom control can often be overused by beginners. It's great for getting close-ups, but zooming in and out too often can make your video difficult to watch. Whenever you can, try moving closer to your subject rather than zooming in.

753 Screenplay
Every digital camcorder has some sort of LCD screen. The screen serves two purposes; you might use it to frame the footage you're about to record, or you can use the screen to watch and review the video you've just shot.

754 Conserving power
LCD screens use up more battery power than viewfinders, so if you need to conserve power, switch off the screen. Luckily, most camcorders will have an onscreen indicator telling you how much battery power is left.

755 Going steady

There are times when you're holding the camcorder in your hand and you just can't keep it steady enough. Use an Image Stabilizer to help you smooth out these shakes. The camcorder automatically compensates for small amounts of unnecessary movement. This rarely results in any drop in image quality.

756 Lighting-up time

For scenes when the background is very bright and the foreground looks so dark you can hardly see any detail, the Backlight Compensation function is a great effect. Use this function to reduce the brightness of the background and bring out detail in the foreground. As the videomaker you'll get a much more attractive shot.

757 The go-between

An effective compromise between shooting on fully Automatic or fully Manual modes, are Program AE (autoexposure) modes. These are available on all digital camcorders. They are Exposure, White Balance, and Shutter Speeds specifically preset for certain conditions, for example: Beach and Ski, Sand and Snow, Low Light, Sports, and Spotlight.

758 Making a move

Getting video and sound off your camcorder onto a computer is very straightforward. Depending on your computer connections, you can use FireWire or USB. Both methods transfer large amounts of data very quickly, and once on your computer you can start editing.

759 Microphone sockets

Sometimes you might need to plug in an external microphone if you need professional-quality sound. Not all digital camcorders have a mic socket, so check this out first. Likewise, headphone sockets aren't on all models, but they're especially useful for monitoring the sound your camcorder is recording.

760 Manual focus

A Manual Focus Ring is found around the lens barrel on more expensive digital camcorders aimed at enthusiasts. The Ring rotates around the lens, and enables you to set the Focus manually.

How to buy a camcorder

761 Set a budget

Decide on your budget. Being realistic will help you make the right decision, as digital camcorders can greatly vary in cost.

762 Check compatibility

Choose a recording format, and decide why. Consider the equipment you already have, and make sure your camcorder will work with it... or you'll be spending a lot of extra money on more new equipment to watch your videos!

763 Your needs

Decide what features you need to have, and those you can really live without. This will help you fix your budget, and decide what kind of videomaker you'll be.

764 On test

Touch and try. Always test out a digital camcorder before buying it. At the very least, you should know how it feels to hold and whether you think it's comfortable.

765 Size matters

Does size matter? In terms of the size of a camcorder, yes it does! It's not that bigger models are better, it's just that smaller ones can be difficult for some people to operate. Buttons can be small and unresponsive on certain models, and there's simply no point having a camcorder that you don't like to use.

766 3CCDs

What is a 3CCD camcorder? The majority of camcorders feature just one CCD (Charge Coupled Device) that turns signals into images. 3CCD models offer greater picture quality, but invariably see a rise in price. Definitely worth considering if you want to make more accomplished movies, but not essential.

767 Free editing

It's very likely you'll get editing software free with your digital camcorder. This can be used to transfer video, audio, and still images off your camcorder onto a computer, and can even let you create DVDs. Check your computer system first for compatibility.

Essential accessories

768 Tripods

The three-legged support you get from a tripod is the best way to shoot rock-solid images. Look out for sturdy build quality and smooth movement, both up and down, and side to side from the head of the tripod. Some tripods have a built-in spirit level so you can be sure your shots are level.

771 Extra storage

Whichever format you record on, it's vital that you have extra capacity with you when shooting. Try to have spare tapes, DVDs, or memory cards with you whenever possible.

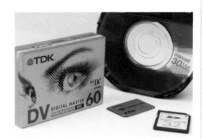

770 Skylight filters

A skylight filter keeps your lens from getting scratched by sand or damaged by dirt but doesn't do anything to alter your images. Filters are available in different sizes to fit your camcorder, and are screwed in front of the lens.

772 Cleaners

A quick dab at your camcorder's lens with an optical cleaning cloth can save you the heartache of watching your footage and realizing you have a stray hair in every single frame!

769 Spare batteries

Having at least one spare, charged battery is essential if you're out and about. That way it's quick and easy to swap over, and you might not miss that classic scene. It's also good to have a stash of several batteries if you're going to do a lot of recording.

773 Light filters

A Neutral Density filter is also essential. It reduces the amount of light entering the camcorder's lens, but doesn't affect the way colors are recorded. It's great for using in very bright conditions, like at the beach or when skiing. A valuable addition to your kit if you know you're going to be shooting a video on vacation—and don't forget to plan for those changing seasons!

Technique
Videomaking is not just about the equipment—a good director can shoot world-beating footage with the right technique, even if the hardware is not the best that money can buy. Here are some basic dos, don'ts, and professional observations.

The basic rules of videomaking

774 Following guidelines

It's understandable how a beginner can feel there are too many essentials to grasp when it comes to videomaking. One thing to remember though, is that most "rules" are really technical "good practice" guides rather than stylistic imperatives.

776 Be selective

Don't feel like you have to record every single moment and event. The best home movies come when you pick the moving, funny, or dramatic moments. Hone your eye by being selective from the outset—and save yourself an editing job later!

775 The lingo

The filmmakers' language is useful to learn when making your own home movies. Once you understand the lingo, then you'll be far more comfortable with what to do and how to do it. Make notes of every technical term you come across in this book and learn it—it's part of the fun, and it will help you think yourself into the role of director and cameraman.

777 Keep it brief

Keep the length of each clip you take down to a minimum. The human eye can process a lot of information very quickly, so you don't have to record in long chunks.

Shot sizes

778 Taking the long shot

A scene usually begins with a long shot (LS). This is because it's the best way of setting the scene. For example, you might begin a vacation video with a long shot of your resort, showing off the long sandy beaches and dazzling views.

780 Close-ups

The next logical step is to add a close-up (CU). This can add even more information, or help focus attention on one particular character—such as the star of your video. Here, you would move closer to your subject, but also use the zoom to get really "tight in" (closely focused) on your main subject: hands, faces, flowers, etc.

781 Zoom with caution

A word on zooming. Overusing the zoom is the most common "mistake" made by beginners. It's not really a mistake though, just a technique that can make it difficult for people to watch your movie. If you want a closer look at something, wherever possible just move closer to it.

782 Add variety

There are variations to all the shot sizes we've mentioned. So you could shoot an extreme close-up (ECU) if you wanted to. This might disorientate your viewer, but then in a nice twist you could use the next shot to zoom out and show what you're looking at.

779 Medium shot

After a long shot you might often cut to a medium shot (MS). This gives a closer look at the action, and offers the viewer more information. So, taking our vacation video one step further, you might choose to look more closely at the vacationers sunning themselves, or buying ice creams.

Videomaking terms

783 Your "frame"

When referring to your "frame," we mean what you can see when you look through the viewfinder, or what you can see on the LCD screen. What you include in the frame is a matter of taste, but can dramatically influence story, character, understanding, and enjoyment.

785 Background

The area at the rear of your video frame is known as the background. Explore the different effects of using it as a visual context for whatever happens in the foreground or center, and as a storytelling device, by setting a scene with the action in the background–and then moving in to find your characters.

786 Center ground

The area in the middle of your video frame is known as the center, and is usually where the majority of the action, or interest, in your video takes place.

784 Foreground

The area at the front of your video frame is known as the foreground. Explore its use by filling it with something, by setting a scene with the action taking place in the background, or as a framing device for action that's happening in the center ground.

787 A cut-in shot

A cut-in can be seen as just another close-up shot. But using it helps you, the videomaker, to tell a story. For example, you have a man walking along the street with a bag. You then have a close-up of the bag. You then film a cut-in of the man reaching inside the bag, and can focus on exactly what's in the bag.

788 Cutaways

Cutaways are great for adding a bit of extra interest to a video, or for helping to tell the story. They're often not essential, but do still have to be related to the story. Your character waits for a friend outside a station. To indicate that someone's running late, you can film a cutaway of a clock to tell the audience what the time is.

789 Panning

Moving the camcorder sideways is known as a pan. So, if you were asked to pan right, you would move the camcorder smoothly toward the right.

790 Tilting

A tilt is when you move the camcorder either up or down. Use this with care and with purpose to avoid disorienting the viewer.

791 Pull-focus shots

You'll need to use manual focus to achieve a pull-focus shot, but they're great for adding emphasis to a video. Using the manual focus, you can make the foreground go fuzzy (out of focus), and the audience will then concentrate on the center or background areas. Or vice versa—make the background fuzzy to emphasize your foreground interest.

792 Jump cuts

Jump cuts are a brilliant example of how there aren't really many firm videomaking rules. Traditionally, a jump cut was seen as a filmmaker's mistake, where one scene doesn't run smoothly with what follows it. For example, if someone was walking toward you, record only a couple of seconds, pause, then record again. Continue this until the person reaches you. When you review the footage, the person would appear to miraculously jump forward toward the camera.

793 Lead room

Lead room is the space you leave in front of your subject for them to move into. Mom skis into shot from the right, and leaves on the left. You should record with space in front of her all the way through the shot.

794 Tracking

A tracking shot is one that involves moving the camcorder to keep the subject in the frame. This will be because your subject (person, car, etc) is moving.

Framing, angles, and eyelines

795 Plan a shot

Once you have your camcorder up and running, you shouldn't necessarily just press the record button. Always try to find time to think about what you're going to record, and how you're going to do it.

796 Composition

Composition is one of the key elements behind getting a great-looking home movie. If you learn a few handy techniques you can make even the most ordinary situations look more interesting.

797 Rule of thirds

The rule of thirds is essential knowledge. Imagine a grid dividing your image into horizontal and vertical thirds (nine squares). To balance what will be competing elements in your shot, attempt to place your subjects on the grid intersections—or devote two thirds of the screen to one element, and a third to another.

798 Framing tip

When framing a subject, especially when this is a person, try to have the bottom of the screen fall midway between joints. A shot that stops at the elbow looks stranger than one that ends at the forearm.

799 A cut above

If you're being creative, you can deliberately cut off the top of someone's head. Say, for example you want to zoom in closer during an interview. The secret is to ensure that it looks deliberate. Many photographers shoot portraits that crop out part of the subject's head to create more dynamic compositions.

800 Spice up long shots

A long shot might look a bit dull without anything else in the frame. Try adding some foreground interest, without distracting from the main focus of the shot.

801 All natural

Most locations will provide you with natural framing aids. Trees and plants are useful for helping to frame a shot, and to add extra interesting elements.

802 Perspective

You might remember perspective from art class. In videomaking, it's vital for creating depth, texture, angles, and for a better-looking video. Instead of filming your subject head-on, which can look flat and boring, try changing the angle. You can then give the viewer more information.

What is depth of field?

803 Acceptable focus

When your lens is focused on a specific point, there will be a distance in front of, as well as behind, that specific point, which will also be in acceptable focus. This area of acceptable focus is known as depth of field.

804 Thinking in thirds

One third of the depth of field area is in front of your focal point, and two thirds is behind it.

805 Zooming in

The depth of field (amount of frame in acceptable focus) decreases as the focal length increases. When you zoom in, less of the frame is in acceptable focus.

806 Angle adjustment

Using a variety of camera angles will make your video more exciting and interesting to watch. Different camera angles can also help you to tell a story better because they can add extra information.

807 Level-headed

Many beginners simply switch on the camcorder, put it up to their eye and start recording. If you did this all the time, all your shots would be from exactly the same height… and that would look monotonous.

808 Point of view

A point of view (POV) shot does exactly what it says: it's filmed as if you're looking through the eyes of your subject. You're seeing what they're seeing.

809 Vary the filming height

Try recording from different heights. Shots from high angles can give a great view looking down on crowd scenes. Low angles, close to the ground, can seem closer to the action—brilliant for when cars or bikes go zipping past.

810 Talking direct to camera

You don't want a person on-camera reading something (like a narration) that's off-camera. This will be unsettling for the viewer, who will feel that the person is being evasive. Get your narrator to learn their lines!

811 Make your mind up

If your subject isn't supposed to look directly at the camcorder, then tell them. It is unnerving for an audience to suddenly have a character gazing directly at them. Alternatively, if you're making a fiction movie, this trick can be used to grab the viewers' attention.

812 Playing with eyelines

You can play with eyelines to help inject drama or comedy into a scene. For example, if one character is looking directly at another, but the other character is looking away, this could be used to suggest an argument, anger, or even someone being coy and bashful.

813 Eye to eye

If you want an audience to realize that two people are looking at each other when you've shot them separately, their eyelines must match. If one character is looking up, then the corresponding character must be looking down.

814 30° (or 30%) rule

When there isn't enough variety between shots, you are breaking the 30° (or 30%) rule. Make sure that when you move the camcorder you do so by 30°. Or, if you change the framing (by zooming), then change it by at least 30 percent.

Crossing the line

815 Improve your filming

The crossing the line rule may seem difficult to grasp at first, but the good news is that once you've got it, you won't have to think about it. And, perhaps more importantly, you'll get much better-looking home movies out of it.

816 Imagine a line

It's known as crossing the line, because you need to imagine a line between your subjects, and to always stay on one side of it.

817 Keep to the same side

Crossing the line is about making things clear for your audience. Imagine watching sport on TV–basketball is a good example. You can see that one team is attacking the basket toward the left of your screen, and the other is attacking the right. This looks natural, because the cameras following the action always follow it from the same side–so, the team attacking left will always look to be attacking that way.

818 Crossing causes confusion

Imagine if the cameras moved without warning, and started filming the game from the other side of the court. The team that was attacking left would now appear to be attacking right. You would feel confused, and find it more difficult to follow the game. If the cameras kept switching to different sides of the court, you'd have no idea which side was attacking which basket.

819 On track

OK, more examples. If you filmed a horse race and stood so the horses ran past you, right to left, but then you moved to the opposite side of the track, so the horses now raced past you left to right, you'd be confused as to which direction the horses were running in when you came to watch that footage.

820 Band aid

You're watching a DVD of your favorite band in concert. The band is always on stage looking out to the audience, and the audience is always in the auditorium looking toward the band on stage. Cross the line, and that natural state will be altered.

821 Chat show

Final example. If you cross the line on a shot of two people chatting, you'll end up with the two people facing the same way. If you don't give your audience any more details, they'll end up thinking that the two people aren't talking to each other at all.

It's vital to cut between shots logically and consistently when dealing with two or more characters. Mixing up the directions from which characters are shot will confuse the viewer and destroy the narrative. Cutting from one to the other from a consistent viewpoint will establish the narrative and lead the viewer into the story.

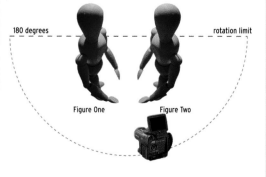

180 degrees   rotation limit

Figure One   Figure Two

Working with equipment

There are thousands of potentially useful accessories and gadgets that can be used with your camcorder to make your shots better or more interesting. Here, we'll cover how to get the best daily use out of the most important gear. Don't worry if you don't fancy buying more equipment—at the end of the section we'll show you how to create some excellent shots and equipment using little more than household objects and ingenuity.

Tripods and monopods

Shaky camerawork is often the province of arty films or gritty TV drama, and it can work well in the right circumstances, but most of the time you're going to want your shots to look smooth and steady, and a tripod or monopod is vital for this.

822 Tripods

As we've already covered, a tripod is the most useful accessory you can buy as it allows you to get rock-steady shots from a variety of angles and heights. But before going out shopping for a tripod, check your camcorder manual to see how much your camcorder weighs, then check that the tripod you're after will support the weight.

823 Cash conscious

Tripods range in price from incredibly inexpensive models to ones costing hundreds of dollars, adorned with all sorts of gadgets and mechanical capabilities. The best ones are actually sold in separate parts—head and legs—allowing you to mix and match what you need.

824 Pan handling

A pan bar is a handle that allows you to move the camera left and right, or tilt it up and down, whilst retaining the stability of the tripod.

825 Buy carefully

Before you set out to buy a tripod, think about how seriously you intend to take your shooting. If you're only going to shoot once or twice a year, don't be seduced by fully-featured expensive models. Look instead for something cheap. It's easy to think that because you've bought an expensive camcorder you need an expensive tripod to do it justice—but that's rarely true.

826 Think about the weight

If you're going to be doing intensive shots with a crew, you'll probably have someone to help carry equipment and can therefore afford a heavier and more durable tripod. But if it's just you, then look for something lighter. Try to find one that comes with a bag, as the strange shape of a collapsed tripod makes it hard to match bag to job.

827 Balancing act

Stabilizers consist of a camcorder platform attached to a free-floating handle that soaks up the jarring of your footsteps. Stabilizers take some getting used to, as you have to carefully counterbalance the weight of your cam using the weights that come with the stabilizer, and you have to learn how to move in a way that allows the platform to float properly. Once you master this, however, you'll be able to carry out stunning tracking shots.

Filters and lens converters

Most camcorders have all sorts of features built-in to change the look of your footage or to cope with adverse shooting conditions such as heavy backlighting. However, sometimes you might find you need something that's not already built-in, which is where filters come in.

828 Filters

Most camcorders have all sorts of features built-in to change the look of your footage or to cope with adverse shooting conditions such as heavy backlighting. However, sometimes you might find you need something that's not already built-in, which is where filters come in.

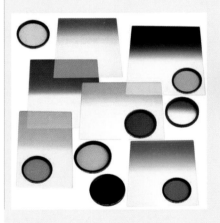 

829 Threads

The lens of almost every camcorder has a filter diameter. This is the size of the thread into which you screw a filter. Look at your camcorder lens—the diameter symbol is a circle with a diagonal line through it. The figure attached to this symbol is the size of filter to shop for.

830 Stepping rings

If you can't find the filter you need in the correct size, you can buy a stepping ring. This has two different-sized threads, one to attach a filter to, and the other to attach to your camcorder through it. The figure attached to this symbol is the size of filter to shop for.

831 Put it in neutral

Neutral density filters are the most commonly used type of filter. They have a gray appearance and are used to reduce the amount of light passing through the lens without affecting color or contrast values. They're useful for regulating uneven lighting conditions and for allowing you to increase depth of field with a wide aperture setting without losing control of your image exposure.

832 Skylight

A skylight filter comes in handy at sporting events or on vacation. It actually has no effect on the image and is essentially just a protective piece of glass that shields your lens from errant softballs or beach sand.

833 Graduated filters

Graduated filters have an effect that is graduated across the lens. For example, they may have a blue tint that slowly fades away to nothing part way down the lens. These are used to enhance parts of images. Those photos with the incredible blue skies for example– do you really think the photographer simply waited for that good a day?

837 Wide-angle convertor

While your camcorder has a function for zooming into a subject, it's rare that it will have a setting to widen your picture. For this, you need a wide-angle convertor lens which screws onto the filter thread. Up to a rating of about x0.5, they will give you a wider picture area. Beyond that size, up to about x0.35, they will start to have a more dramatic distorting effect called "fish eye," in which items at the edge of the frame appear to bend in toward the center.

834 Polarizing filters

Polarizing filters are used primarily for reducing glare and flare from reflective subjects, although they can also be used to enhance it. A polarizing filter lets you film through windows or water on sunny days. Where normally you'd get a blazing white reflection, a polarizing filter will let you look through the glass or the water.

835 Softeners

Softening lenses reduce the sharpness of an image slightly, without throwing it completely out of focus. They are ideal for portrait shots as they soften or remove minor blemishes and wrinkles.

836 Vignetting

One small problem with attaching zoom or wide-angle convertor lenses to camcorders is vignetting, in which the addition of length to the lens barrel causes the camcorder to try to see through the side of the filter, creating a tunnel vision effect. This can be avoided by zooming slightly.

Basic lighting

Most basic shoots don't require any lighting, and it's possible that you'll never need to light your video. Having said that, your camcorder is, primarily, a tool for working with light, so it's important to know some of the basics of lighting just in case. Imagine you're asked to film someone's wedding, or an important presentation—if the lighting is bad, you need to know how to make it better.

838 Don't make your own

People often think that video or film lights can be made cheaply using garden lamps or security lights. This is a mistake, as these sort of lights aren't "balanced," and tend to have a tinge to them that, although unnoticeable to the naked eye, will definitely affect your video, resulting in "color casts." Natural light or proper video lights are the best sources of illumination to work with.

839 Redheads and blonds

The most commonly used type of video light is the redhead, also known as the focusing reflector. These have significantly more wattage than household bulbs, and are balanced to the same blueish tinge as natural light, rather than the more orange tinge of an ordinary bulb. Higher wattage focusing reflectors are known as "blonds."

840 Key lighting

If you do need to light your scene, there are three main styles of lighting that can be used in different combinations. The first is the key light. This is your primary light source for what you're shooting, and is used to drive out darkness and place realistic shadows. This is where the terms low-key and high-key come from. Low-key lighting is of a lesser brightness and intensity than high-key. Your key light is usually shone from the front or front side of your subject.

841 Fill lighting

When your key light is placed, you'll probably find that the shadows it creates are more intense than you want, illuminating most of your subject perfectly, but creating a few shrouded patches, such as the eyes or nose. Your fill light is placed to the opposite angle of your key to fill these shadows, but is of a lesser intensity so as not to completely override the key. Often a good fill lighting effect can be achieved by facing the light away from the subject and bouncing it back toward the subject with a reflector.

842 Kicker lights

Lastly, you have the kicker. With your key and fill in position, it's possible that both subject and background are so evenly lit as to appear flat. The kicker brings some depth back in by "kicking" your subject out from the background. Usually placed low and to the rear of the subject, the kicker adds some light to the edges of your subject, making it more clearly defined from the background.

843 Three-point lighting

The use of key, fill, and kicker in conjunction is called three-point lighting, and is handy for almost any type of lighting situation. The concept can be used with more than three lights, or you can use two-point or single-point lighting in less demanding situations.

845 Reflectors

Reflectors are used to bounce light to where it's needed. Made of a reflective fabric, they normally fold down to a small and easily portable size. The most common reflectors are white/silver and white/gold. The white is a basic reflector used for bouncing light from the sun or a luminaire at your subject, while the silver or gold sides are used to alter the light quality as well as reflecting it. The gold "warms" the light the most.

844 Softbox

A softbox is used to spread and diffuse the light from a single source. Made of springy fabric, they collapse for easy packing. Fitted over a luminaire they will spread the light as well as soften it, producing even lighting conditions with mild shadows for a very natural look.

846 Barn doors

Barn doors are hinged metal flaps that fit onto your lights, allowing you to restrict the spread of the light without reducing its intensity. Using barn doors you can create a very directional light source.

847 Snoots

A snoot is a conical version of barn doors. You can restrict the diameter of the beam, allowing you to create a spotlight.

Basic sound recording

Good pictures are nice, but combined with good sound they become great. This section will teach you the basics of recording good sound and tell you what equipment you might need if you want to get ambitious with your audio.

848 Audio dub

The first and easiest thing you can do to improve your camcorder sound is to use the audio dub facility present on all DV camcorders. Ordinarily, your cam records 16-bit audio onto two channels. By switching this to 12-bit, however, you leave a channel free onto which you can dub music or narration onto your tapes. Simply plug a microphone or a stereo/minidisk player into the mic socket on your camcorder, and select audio dub from the menu.

849 Headphones

If you're going to record separate sound to add to your video during editing, you'll want to invest in some good headphones to monitor your recording. Headphones can be either closed, which let in no external noise and are therefore better for monitoring, or open, which let you hear the world around you and are much safer for shooting when you're out and about.

850 Destination

You'll also need to think about where your sound is going to end up. Once upon a time separate audio was recorded onto tape, but these days far better results can be achived using minidisk or an MP3. These devices also have the added advantage of being more easily transferred to your editing system than tape.

851 Shotgun

Of course, you'll also need to find the microphone best suited to your recording. Shotgun mics are long and thin and easy to use by hand or when attached to a boom. The pickup pattern on them captures sound mainly from the front, which means you'll get only the sound you point them at.

852 Cardioid

Cardioid mics are the most common variety, and have a heart-shaped pickup pattern where most sound is picked up from the front, but some is also taken from the sides. These are very handy for recording ambient noise that adds interest and authenticity to your soundtrack.

853 Lavalier

Lavalier mics are the ones you see on TV clipped to people's ties, and are therefore often called tie-clip mics. Brilliant for picking up speech, lavaliers can be very useful during long interviews or when recording monologues.

854 Get as close as possible

The most important rule for recording good sound is to get as close as possible to the source of the sound. The closer you are, the cleaner and louder the sound will be. If it's inconvenient to put the camcorder and its microphone close to your subject, then try to record the sound separately by having a mic much closer to the subject than the camera.

855 Boom

The best way of getting your mic close to your source is by using a boom. These are long poles (sometimes called fishing poles) with a mic on the end that can be held directly above the source of the sound while still being too high to appear in shot. It's easy to make a boom from a fishing pole or aluminum tubing if you want to save money.

856 Shield the mic from wind

Wind disturbance is the most common interference with your sound, with pops and rustles being recorded as the wind hits the mic. You can use a wind-cut mode to reduce this, but on most camcorders this involves switching to mono sound recording. Instead, keep the camcorder recording in stereo and purchase a windshield made from foam or fur that fits over your microphone.

857 Listen for disturbances

Your mind is very good at screening out extraneous noises picked up by your ears, but that's a talent your camcorder doesn't have. Listen extra hard when recording for all the background noises (airplanes, the hum of fluorescent lights, etc) that will be picked up by your microphone.

858 Tapped up

If you're planning to add sound to your video at the editing stage, it's important to be able to sync it with a visual cue. You might think that you'll just start the words when someone's lips start moving, but it will never match. Get someone to snap a clapper board shut or tap the top of the microphone in shot, and then line the sound up to the movement in post-production.

859 Go wild

Silence is rarely actually silence, and ambient noise is never easy to recreate. A wildtrack is sound recorded independently of your picture that has nothing to do with your story and is used for realistic video soundtrack. Even an empty room has certain acoustic properties—even if it's silent it still doesn't sound the same as it would if you simply shot it with the volume turned down. A wildtrack will capture these properties, or the general ambient noise of any location you shoot in, and when mixed with your video, will make it sound authentic.

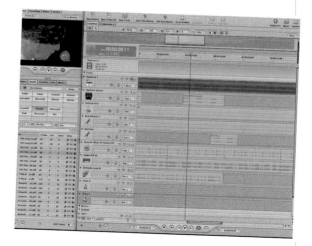

Audio- and video-editing software works on a timeline principle, showing every element of your work graphically. You can line up audio cues visually in your edit suite.

What can I video?

Now that you know what camcorder, accessories, and kit you should have, here are a few ideas on what you might use all that precious stuff for.

Vacations

860 Which vacation?

There are a couple of main vacation scenarios. First is a break where you just want a record of your visit, and the second is a trip of a lifetime where you want to document as much as you can. The latter takes careful planning, and a lot of specialist equipment. Here, we're going to concentrate on the standard vacation.

861 Stick to the highlights

For an average family break, try to cut down the amount of equipment you take—you don't want it to rule your trip. You're trying to relax, remember. Try restricting yourself to recording the highlights, such as special days out.

862 Essential kit

The essential kit should include the camcorder, a few tapes, cards or discs, a couple of batteries (one can be charging while the other's in use), a mains charger, and a secure bag to keep it all in.

863 Check voltage

Check the voltage in use where you're on vacation, so you can use the charger to power up those batteries.

864 The tripod stays home

A tripod can be unnecessary baggage. Instead, try using natural supports such as walls, fences, and tables—not quite so adaptable, but better than carrying around awkward bags.

865 Insurance check

Check your home contents and vacation insurance polices. Is your camcorder covered, or will you need to take out separate cover? Most leading insurers will offer cover for specific costly items.

866 Do some groundwork

Consider what you're shooting, plan it in advance where possible, and keep shot lengths short for maximum impact. You don't need to document all 7 or 14 days!

867 Add variety

Shooting into the sun will lead to overexposed or bleached-out looking shots when you're using the camcorder's auto settings. Look for areas of light and shade to give your video variety.

868 People, not places

Make sure you video friends and family doing activities. Videos of buildings and beaches can look a little dull. Vary the height and angle of shots to add interest to the video.

869 Visual clues

Use road and town signs as a visual reference. They can also act as impromptu titles for the video, so you don't have to add them later when you're editing.

Weddings

870 The big day

Weddings are difficult and important events, so plan everything you can down to the last detail. You won't have any spare time on the day.

871 Ask permission

As a matter of courtesy find out in advance that it's alright for you to set up your camcorder where you need to. Priests and officiators often have control over a ceremony venue.

A WEDDING SEQUENCE

872 Set the scene

Record guests as they congregate. Mix shots of people milling around outside and inside the venue, grab a few shots of nervous relatives, and do a few interviews with key figures.

873 Get in position

If you're recording the ceremony on just one camcorder, position it so that you can capture the action in one fluid movement.

874 Make an entrance

Here we are fixed on the entrance to the church, ready to capture the bride as she comes in.

875 Walk on by

Follow the bride as she comes down the aisle with her party and arrives at the altar to meet her groom. But do take care not to be the center of attention or to spoil the moment by getting in the way!

876 Create atmosphere

Find the time to grab a few reaction shots of the guests as they comment on the bride's dress. Close-ups of smiles and of the odd tear help to add atmosphere.

877 The happy couple

Now it's time to focus on the ceremony, so make sure the position of your camcorder allows you to focus in on the happy couple and the priest or officiator.

878 Stay with that shot

You should now be able to relax slightly and use the same shot to record the entire ceremony... bar the unexpected, of course!

879 Shifting focus

If you're allowed to, stick with the wedding party and record the signing of the register or official documents. If not, concentrate on atmospheric shots of the congregation. Mix up medium and close-up shots.

880 Change position

Change location and get to the exit of the church so that you can record the couple coming back down the aisle and leaving–much better than running down the aisle in the happy couple's wake.

881 Mix 'n' match

Let the official photographer do their job and take the all-important commissioned stills. Grab a few shots of the picture-taking, guests' reactions, confetti throwing, and the happy couple's departure.

884 Knowing when to stop

Many professional wedding videomakers capture the couple's first dance and the first few tunes from the band or disco. After that it can degenerate into drunken relative dancing! So that's up to you.

882 Speeches

When it comes to recording speeches, you should find a position that will allow the viewer to see the speaker, as well as enough of the audience to see, as well as hear, their reaction.

883 Place your microphone

Think about how close you need to be for your microphone (built-in to the camcorder, or external, if you're using it) to pick up the speeches. Not all speakers project their voices well. With some non-directional mics you may record the conversation of the people around you, so make sure they're being polite!

CAPTURING SPORTS ACTION

885 Action stations

Choosing to record a sporting event is a popular videomaking occasion. There is a wide range of subjects to pick from and, because there's always action involved, you're guaranteed to get some great recording opportunities.

886 Call it a day

A day out at a Grand Prix or a horse racing meet is a fantastic chance to capture fast-moving action in atmospheric surroundings.

887 Team effort

If you're a member of a football, baseball, or hockey team, then you can help to video games. These can then be used to help improve performance, by showing your teammates what they're doing right and wrong.

888 Team tactics

You might also want to video your opponents before you play them, getting your colleagues some invaluable insights into how they might approach the game.

889 Self-improvement

Videos can help in individual sports, too. Cyclists, boxers, golfers, and tennis players can develop their performances by looking at improving a serve or a swing, or at which stages of an event they lose drive or impetus.

890 Smooth operater

Because fast-moving action can be just that—fast—use a tripod to make sure your footage is as smooth as possible. And practice any fast pans or tilts in advance.

891 Expect the unexpected

Follow the action as smoothly as possible from beginning to end. You're not always sure how events might unfold, so be on the lookout to capture as much as possible.

892 Leave plenty of room

Remember that phrase Lead Room? It's vital with sports that you leave enough space in front of the action for your subject to move into to "tell the story" to the viewer.

893 Put it into context

Use long shots to establish your location. The audience needs to know where you are and what they are meant to be watching before they can appreciate the onscreen action.

894 Get on down

A variety of angles will mean your footage will look as exciting as the action you're recording. Get down low when a car or bike whizzes past. It will seem so much faster.

895 On autopilot

In many cases, you can use the camcorder's auto settings, as this means you won't have to waste time setting focus and exposure.

896 Manual for close-ups

However, manual focus and exposure settings are invaluable when it's essential to get good close-ups. Practice and set up the manual focus and exposure modes in advance of shooting.

897 Blur can be good

Sometimes, blurred footage is actually a great video effect. Don't fear trailing or slightly out of focus shots if they add drama or tension.

898 Higher shutter speeds

Higher shutter speeds capture fast-moving action more smoothly. So if your camcorder has them, try using them.

899 Don't cross the line!

Make use of that Crossing the Line term you learned earlier. Shooting a car race and breaking that 180° rule, will leave your audience confused as to which direction the traffic's headed in!

Auoiding the shakes

Dolly, or tracking, shots are fairly long shots that follow a subject. Commonly used in video and filmmaking, in order to achieve a shake-free shot, the camera is usually mounted on a form of wheeled cart.

900 Wheely good ideas

Of course, you can carry out dolly shots using just about anything with wheels. The lack of tracks limits you to smooth terrain only, but there are still plenty of times when a homemade dolly will come in handy. The most common substitute dolly is a wheelchair. Sit your camera operator in it and push. Just about everything can be used as a substitute dolly, from shopping carts to skateboards, depending on the height that's needed.

901 The dolly zoom

As soon as people have a dolly, they want to do a dolly zoom. This is the unsettling effect used in Hitchcock's *Vertigo* and Spielberg's *Jaws*, in which the background seems to move, looming up behind a stationary subject in the foreground. Variously known as the contrazoom, trombone shot, or occasionally the zolly, dolly zooms take advantage of the way that a zoom lens brings the background closer, not by moving the lens but by compressing the middle ground. This has the effect of altering perspective without changing the subject size—completely the opposite of what the human eye expects to see.

902 Experimental shots

The procedure for a dolly zoom is actually quite simple, but the timing is difficult to get right as the speeds of the dolly and the zoom need to be fairly close to each other. Place a subject within a few feet of your lens, with an interesting background some distance away. Trees or buildings work better than a flat landscape. Using your wheelchair dolly, move backward slowly, away from your subject, while zooming in at a speed relative to the backward movement. Although the effect is noticeable in the movement of the background, the trick is to concentrate on your foreground subject, keeping them the right size in the frame.

903 Physical panning

If you haven't got a tripod it can be difficult to carry out panning shots smoothly by hand, but it's not impossible. In the same way that there are physical techniques for lifting heavy objects, there are physical techniques for panning, too.

904 Start at the end

In order to pan smoothly without a tripod, you need to move your body in certain ways. Start by facing where you want the pan to end. Position yourself in a comfortable, natural shooting position and anchor your feet.

908 Walk like an Egyptian

When walking with a camcorder you need to make a bit of a fool of yourself in order to keep the shot smooth. The idea is to turn your body into a shock absorber whilst adjusting your gait to produce minimal movement.

909 Crouching cameraman, hidden movement

First you need to curl your body into a slight crouch in an attempt to centralize your weight and soften your motion. Then bend your knees slightly and try to keep them bent as the flex will soak up some of your footfalls.

905 Set up the start

Now you have the action set up and ready to go at the point where the pan will start following it from. Put the camcorder to your eye and carefully twist yourself backwards from the waist into position to start the pan, while leaving your feet placed exactly as they were.

906 Action...

Just before the action starts, slightly bend your knees and slowly unwind your body to pan along with what you're shooting.

907 ... and pan!

By loading all the pressure onto your muscles from the start and unwinding to a comfortable position, you'll accomplish a much smoother pan.

912 Assume the position

When shooting from a stationary position, keep your elbows tucked in to your body as close as you can to keep the camera stable. Better yet, rest your elbows on something solid.

913 Zoom focus

When preparing a shot, zoom your camcorder in slightly before you adjust the focus. Once you've got the image sharp, zoom back out to the original position–the image will only get sharper. This is a trick used by professional camera operators all the time, and is equally useful on basic camcorders.

910 On the move

As you walk, lengthen your stride slightly–not enough to lurch, but enough that each step becomes very careful and deliberate. Place one foot in front of the other as if walking along a beam, to minimize side-to-side motion.

911 Hold your breath

Although impossible for long walks with the camcorder, on short walks it's worth trying to hold your breath. Inhalations expand your chest and lift your shoulders, taking the camcorder with it. The exhale then reverses the effect.

Video Editing

Editing your work
In this section you'll learn how to edit your videos, with a guide to the equipment, creative skills, and basic procedures for using two commonplace video-editing programs available on the market—both of which are free! If you learn to edit your videos, you can make your vacation movies more interesting, add captions to birthday parties, and add titles to school plays. And if you're making a fiction movie, you can create timing and tension in the same way that Hollywood does.

Editing principles

So, you've got your footage on tape in your camcorder and you're ready to start editing. The next set of tips will tell you how to prepare for the edit and what sort of cuts and joins you can make.

914 Be constructive

People often focus their attention on the destructive part of editing, simply working out which shots are extraneous and hacking them out. Try to think constructively—editing is as much about how you join up the footage you want as it is about removing the footage you don't.

915 Visualization

Before you start shooting, try drawing a storyboard that shows all your camera angles and how one shot joins to the next. This will save you hours of time in the editing room by giving you a blueprint for your edit, and will also save on wasted tape by making sure you know in advance what you do and don't need to shoot.

916 Get coverage

Coverage is the professional term for getting all the shots that an editor might need to work with. It doesn't mean shooting everything in sight, but it does mean making sure they have shots that identify the location and the participants, known as establishing shots, as well as those containing all the action.

917 Masters and cutaways

As well as establishing shots it's also a good idea to get a master shot and some cutaways. The master is a wide shot of the whole scene in a single take, and cutaways are various close-ups on items or people in the scene. If you have these then you can assemble a workable version of the scene should anything go wrong with the more complicated version you storyboard. That's why master shots are sometimes called safety shots. They're insurance.

918 Timeline editors

There are two main types of video-editing software. The first is the timeline style. In this, all your video and audio is placed on specific tracks you create for them, and the length of each shot is represented by the length of the shot icon on the timeline. The advantage of timelines is that they make it easy to see how your project fits together and to do cutaways. The uppermost element on a timeline is what plays, so a two second clip placed on a timeline track above and halfway along a 10 second clip will mean that you'll automatically cut from the 10 second clip to the two second one and back again.

919 Storyboard editors

Better suited to beginners are storyboard-editing layouts, in which all the clips are represented by a single icon and shown in sequence. A storyboard simply shows shot one next to shot two, and so on. You can then rearrange shots by dragging them into different orders.

920 In the bin

Bins are where you keep all the files associated with your video. They are displayed onscreen in your video-editing software and help you keep yourself organized by creating a filing system. For example, you could have a bin for video clips, another for audio clips, a third for effects, and another for titles. You can find the arrangement that suits you, but do try to use the bins, as they break complicated projects down into easy-to-handle chunks.

921 Cut for meaning, then for feel

This is a maxim used by professional editors and it means exactly what it says. When you first cut together a scene, concentrate on making sure it says everything it has to say, then work on adding the shots that get across the feelings it should convey. For example, a scene with lots of people shouting and looking angry will convey the feelings, but not the crux of the conflict in the scene. You need to get the argument assembled coherently before your audience can make sense of the characters' behavior.

922 Context

Pudovkin and Kuleshov, two Russian editors working in the 1920s, discovered that the same shot of a man's face was interpreted differently by audiences depending on what was shown before or after it. Using shots of a child, a bowl of soup, and a coffin, the same image of the face was made to convey parental pride, hunger, and grief. Keep this in mind when editing—you make the shots convey whatever you want them to by linking them to other shots. On their own they can be anything, in your hands they can be what you want them to be.

923 Continuity editing

There are three main styles of editing. Continuity is the most common, and its purpose is to truncate real time into screen time without the audience noticing that anything has been edited. For example, a man may take five minutes to make a cup of coffee, but careful editing of a kettle being filled, coffee being spooned into a cup, the kettle spout whistling, water being poured, and the man drinking can turn those five minutes into 30 seconds, without spoiling the audience's illusions.

924 Parallel editing

Parallel editing is useful for building tension in your audience. Say, for example, you have two separate sequences such as a groom arriving at a church and a bride getting ready for the big day. They may have taken place at different times, but if you cut back and forth from one to the other you both truncate the time and relate the two sequences to each other, allowing your audience to get excited about how one sequence affects the other. You still need to arrange the shots in the same order as you would with continuity editing, but you also cut between the two sequences at regular intervals.

LR:000002

FN.73 9696 5616+00   02:04:07:05.

LR:000001

FN.73 7669 9771+07   01:02:27:14.

Here's a logical sequence of edits: at the beginning of the scene, our two protagonists are seen together in a medium two-shot; next, the camera zooms in to focus on their conversation; last, is the reaction shot from a third character—in this movie, the antagonist.

925 Montage editing

Sometimes referred to as collision editing, montage editing states that two seemingly unrelated shots, known as thesis and antithesis, can be combined to make clear something that is apparent in neither of them: synthesis. For example, someone in a bright office working frantically, followed by the same person slumped in a dark bar looking drunk, will combine to suggest the sort of toll hard work is taking on the character.

926 Motivation

When cutting from one shot to another, try to find motivation— a reason to cut from one shot to the next. It could be a noise offscreen, a movement onscreen, even a simple flicker in a character's eyeline. Having something trigger or motivate a cut makes your editing feel more seamless.

927 Hold it right there!

Think about how long you need to hold a shot onscreen for in order for your audience to make sense of it. Something likely to be familiar to your audience, such as a simple house on a street, needs much less time onscreen than, say, an ornate palace.

Video Editing

Getting rid of unnecessary footage (mistakes, boring moments, and footage that just doesn't look good) helps to make a better-looking movie. You'll get more satisfaction watching it, and so will your friends. But trimming clips isn't the only aspect of editing. You can add titles and effects, such as dissolves and crossfades, so clips flow seamlessly into one another. You can even include a new soundtrack, with music or narration.

Editing might seem like a complex subject but it's not. It's just a whole new range of things you can do to make better home movies. Here we're going to look at two editing software programs for your home computer. You'll find there's software to suit every budget and ability.

Over the next few chapters we'll teach you the basics of editing with two different programs. iMovie (Mac) and Movie Maker (Windows) are designed for beginners and are provided free with most computers–they're therefore most likely to be the first editing programs you encounter.

iMovie

Apple's iMovie application comes bundled with Macs as part of the iLife suite that is included with the Mac Operating System.

928 What is iMovie?

iMovie is Apple's entry level, non-linear editing software. It gives you a range of basic tools for editing your movies, together with some fun special effects and atmospheres that you can use to add drama to your existing shots–e.g. lightning flashes, a snowstorm, and "old movie" textures.

929 What can it do?

iMovie provides the basic tools for capturing video from your camcorder into your computer, cutting it to length, reordering it, adding special effects, titles, and soundtracks, and exporting it back to tape, onto DVD, onto the Internet, or even to a video-equipped cellphone.

930 Why do we like it?

iMovie is designed for beginners and is incredibly easy to use, yet it's still capable of producing results of a very high standard. Films made using iMovie have even made it into movie theaters and the Cannes Film Festival. Furthermore, because iMovie is well integrated with the rest of iLife, it makes it very easy to use stills and audio from iPhoto and iTunes within your video, and export projects to iDVD.

933 In the bin

The bin varies according to what icon is selected on the menu palette, and shows all the relevant files for the selected icon. In clip mode it shows all the video clips you've captured; in audio mode it shows all the tunes in your audio library; in transitions mode it shows the various transitions you can apply to your footage. To incorporate files from the bin into your video, drag them from the bin onto the timeline.

934 The Menu palette

The Menu palette is displayed beneath the bin and is used to select files that are shown in the bin. When you click the icon on the palette that relates to something customizable, such as a transition, it will change the bin to display the controls used to customize the transition, as well as showing you all the transitions that are available.

931 Window display

The first thing you need to be aware of in iMovie is the display window. This is where you watch the video that you're working with. It can be used to play clips from the bin or the timeline, and the little handles on the timeline built into the display window can be dragged to where you want a particular clip to begin and end, making it easy to trim video clips to the size you want.

932 Timeline

iMovie's timeline displays your video and audio channels, and the length of the clips you have on them, giving your project a jigsaw-like appearance. Using the timeline you can see how different pieces of footage fit together. If that's too complicated, the timeline can be turned into a storyboard that shows a simpler linear progression of clips.

935 Capturing video

Plug your camcorder's FireWire output into your computer's FireWire socket, then click the toggle beneath the display window so that it moves from the scissors icon to the camera icon. iMovie can now control your camcorder.

936 Importing video

Use the Play button onscreen to play through the tape in your camcorder. When the piece of video you want to capture starts to run on the screen, click the Import button and iMovie will bring that video into the clip bin—when you reach the end of the clip, hit the Import button again to stop the procedure. Carry on doing this until all the clips you want have been imported to the clip bin.

937 Putting video on the timeline

Click the toggle back from the camcorder to the scissors icon to enter iMovie's editing mode, then select the first clip you want to use by clicking and dragging it from the bin onto the timeline.

938 Viewing the timeline

Just above the timeline are two icons—a filmstrip and a clock. If you click the clock icon, your timeline will be displayed as differently sized chunks of separate video and audio. This view is good for fitting together intricate sequences and adjusting clip lengths. The little arrow with the line coming out of it is called the playhead—its position on the timeline indicates the location of what's shown in the display window.

939 Viewing the storyboard

If you click the filmstrip icon, the timeline turns into a storyboard–this displays only a sequence of icons representing the clips you've edited, but not their duration or audio tracks. This mode is handy for an overview, and for quickly adding transitions by simply dragging and dropping them between icons.

940 Trimming clips

Sometimes you need to shorten a clip. There are two ways to do this. The first is to click the end of the clip on the timeline and drag it to the left, until it's where you want it to end. To fine-tune this, use the left and right cursor keys to drag the clip back or forward one frame at a time. Alternatively, you can click on the blue bar at the bottom of the display window and drag the two yellow arrows inwards. This lets you trim the beginning and end of the clip to specific lengths, useful if you only want the middle piece of the clip.

941 Restore, duplicate, and paste

Trimming the clip doesn't mean you can't also use it at full length elsewhere on your timeline. You can drag the clip back to full length by reversing what you did in Tip 940. You can also copy the clip by clicking on it, then selecting Copy from the Edit menu. Next, you can paste the copy onto the timeline by moving the playhead to the point where you want to insert the video and selecting Paste from the Edit menu.

942 Creating titles

Having trimmed and assembled all your clips you can then add a title. Click the T icon in the Menu palette and select the font you want to use from the list. Then type the title you want into the boxes provided.

943 Adjust the title

Drag the slider back and forth between the big and little "A" until the text in the preview window is the size you want it to be in proportion to the rest of your video. Then click the box marked Color. A wheel will appear showing various colors in different tones—click the part of the wheel that matches the color you want your title to be.

946 Playing with pictures

An advantage of iMovie is that it works with a photo management program called iPhoto and lets you add stills to your video. Click the photos icon in the Menu palette to display a list of all the photos in your iPhoto library. Click on a photo and adjust its display size and screen time duration by dragging the blue blob along the two sliders above the list.

944 Style it up

Scroll through the list of text effects and choose a style that suits your video. By clicking an effect, you can see it previewed in the window at the top of the bin.

947 The Burns' effect

The Ken Burns' effect, named after the man who used it so effectively in the PBS Civil War documentary, adds a bit of life to stills by panning across them or around them. It's a great way of compensating for the lack of motion in a still photo. The effect can be turned off by clicking the blue tickbox.

945 What a drag

Having chosen a font, size, color, and style, click the icon in the list and drag it down to the timeline. Once you've dropped it onto the timeline, a few moments will pass as iMovie prepares a preview which will let you see the text as part of your video project.

948 Adding a still to the timeline

Once you're happy with the photo you've chosen, click and drag it to the timeline the same way you dragged the text. If you've used the Ken Burns' effect there will be a slight delay as iMovie renders the photo.

949 Adding audio

Step 1: Now we're going to add music and narration to the video. The first step is to turn off the preexisting audio so that it doesn't interfere with your fine-tuning of the new audio. At the end of the timeline, click the blue tickbox next to the audio track. When the box is gray and unticked, the audio track is still present, but won't play back.

Step 2: Click the audio icon to display the contents of your iTunes library, then click the song you want and hit the play button to listen to it.

Step 3: Drag the playhead along the timeline to the spot where you want the music to start, then hit the place at playhead button. There will be a slight delay while iMovie converts the song to a format it can use, then the music will appear in the audio channel that still has a tick in its box.

950 Adding narration

If you want to add narration, select the target audio track to record the narration by unclicking the tickbox on the other audio track, then plug a microphone into your computer's mic input, hit the red record button next to the microphone display in the audio bin, and begin speaking. When you're done, hit the record button again to stop recording. If you make a mistake, drag the playhead back to the beginning and repeat the process to record over the first attempt.

951 Adjusting audio levels

You can adjust the audio levels on-the-fly so that different sections of the same audio channel have different volumes. In the View menu, select Show Audio Waveforms and Show Clip Volume Levels. The waveform displays the peaks and troughs of the audio, while the black line in the middle is the volume. Drag the line up or down for an overall increase or decrease. Alternatively, click at two different spots on the line to make pegs appear—you can drag these pegs up and down, and the volume line between them will adjust to correspond. For example, to fade the audio down slowly, create the first peg where the fade will start, and the second where it will end, then drag the second peg downward to the level you want it to end at.

952 Selecting transitions

Transitions are changes from one clip to the next. A straight cut is a type of transition, but the ones that appear when you click the transitions icon are rather more stylized. Click on the transitions icon and scroll through the list until you find one that you like.

953 Adjust the duration

A transition with a duration of 10 seconds won't work if the clips on either side of it are shorter than 10 seconds, so you'll need to drag the blue blob on the speed slider to a length that fits between your two clips.

954 Add the transition

The easiest way to add your transition is to switch into the storyboard mode, as this displays the clips as simple icons. Drag your chosen transition from the menu and hover it over the icons and they'll slide apart to accommodate the transition. Release the mouse button to drop the transition into place.

955 iDVD integration

DVD is now the most common way to distribute home movies. Add chapter marks in your project by clicking the iDVD icon in the Menu palette, dragging the playhead to the point where you want a chapter break to occur, then hitting the add chapter button.

956 Saving your work

It's rare that you'll be able to edit and export an entire project in one go, so it's important to save your work as you go along. In the File menu, select Save As and give it a simple, recognizable title.

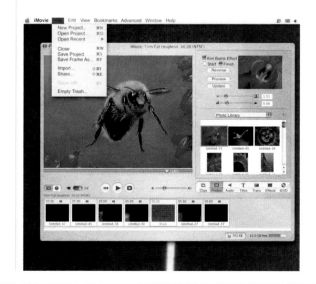

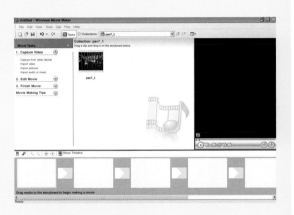

957 Windows Moviemaker

This software program is from Microsoft and has been designed for beginners. It has a simple layout (or interface as it's known) and is for a PC—it's not compatible with a Mac. The big advantage is that it comes with Windows Vista, in the accessories folder under your Start button.

Step 1: Capture video
As long as your computer has a FireWire port you can plug in a camcorder, and select Capture from Video Camera from the menu at the left of the screen.

Step 2: Name your video clips
MovieMaker will prompt you to name your video clips, and ask if you want to capture the whole tape automatically, or bits of it manually.

Step 3: Load additional footage
If you want to include footage you've captured previously, or already have on disk from another source, just select File/Import Into Collections and it will be loaded into the Collection window.

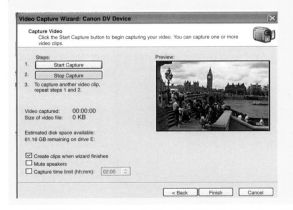

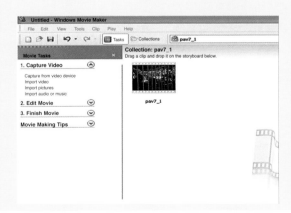

Step 4: Drop a clip onto the storyboard
Grab one of your shots from the Collections window and drag it into the first empty slot on the storyboard (at the bottom of the screen).

Step 5: Add another clip
Now drag in another shot next to it. This creates your first edit. Hit play (just below the monitor on the right hand side of the screen) and your two shots will play through.

Step 6: Change the order of clips
You can drag in as many shots as you like, and change the order in which they appear by simply dragging them backward or forward on the storyboard.

Step 7 – Add a transition
If you don't want a straight cut between your shots, you can easily add a different transition. Choose Video Transitions from the drop-down list above the Collections window, and you're offered a massive array of transition effects.

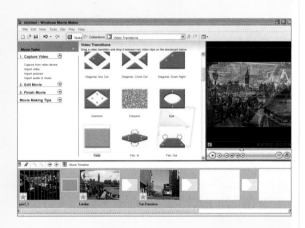

Step 8: Adding a fade
By far the most useful feature is the Fade. Simply drag it to the small box between two of your shots, and when you play back the production, the fade will be in place.

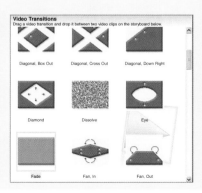

Step 9: Trim your edits
We now want to tighten up our edits a little, and that's difficult with the Storyboard view. Click the Show Timeline button just above the storyboard, and Movie Maker switches to a Timeline view.

Step 11: Special effects
Movie Maker comes with a range of effects–familiarize yourself with them by experimenting with a copy of some footage.

Step 12: Select an effect
Adding effects is simple. Just select Video Effects from the drop-down menu above the Collections window, choose an effect, and drag it onto a clip.

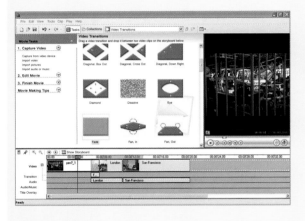

Step 13: Changing an effect
If you don't like what you see, right-click on the clip, choose Video Effects, and you can remove it again.

Step 10: Shorten a clip in timeline view
Here, you can trim clips by simply placing your cursor between two shots, and clicking and dragging. The monitor shows the frame that's being moved, so you can easily find the point at which you want to cut in or out.

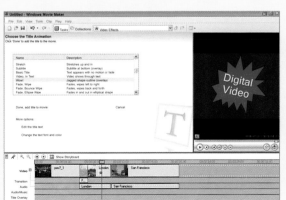

Step 14: Adding titles
In order to add titles, captions, or credits, simply pick Titles and Credits from the Tools menu.

Step 15: Choosing a title
A wizard appears allowing you to add basic titles.

Step 16: Adding music
To add music (or other sound effects) just select Import Audio or Music from the menu to the left of the screen.

Step 17: Selecting audio clips
Now locate any audio clips you have on your hard drive (these can often have a suffix such as MP3, AIFF, Windows Media, or AAC).

Step 18: Insert audio clip
These audio files then appear in the Collections window, and can be dragged onto the audio track (the second track from the bottom of the timeline).

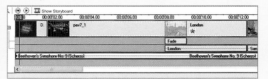

Step 19: Complete your video
When you're ready to produce your finished video, MovieMaker offers a number of options under the Finish Movie menu on the left of the screen.

Step 20: Choose a format
You can create an email, a CD, a Web page, or a DV tape. Each selection has an easy-to-follow wizard to lead you through the process.

Video output

Sharing your video

Finally we get to the best bit, the culmination of all your work—sharing your video with an audience, be it family, friends, or strangers on the other side of the world. In this section we'll give you a few pointers about how your video should be prepared, and tell you how to use the most common methods of distribution.

958 Things to think about

Before you begin exporting your video, it's important to work out a few things, most notably who is your audience and where are they? There are certain guidelines for submitting video to producers or TV companies that don't apply to family and friends, and of course, there are different TV systems in operation around the world that need to be taken into account.

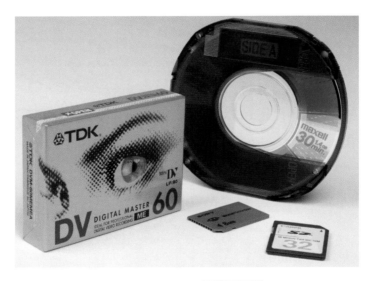

960 SECAM

Sequential Couleur Avec Memoire is the television system used in France. A version of it known as MESECAM is also used in the Middle East. If you're planning to send tape or DVD to these countries, you need to adjust the preferences setting in your NLE system to the correct television standard in order to make the finished result compatible.

959 At any rate

NTSC is the television system in use in the US and Japan. It has a horizontal resolution of 525 lines, and a frame rate of 30 frames per second. In the UK, Australia, and most of Europe, televisions and VCRs use the Phase Alternating Line (PAL) system, in which 625 lines of horizontal resolution are displayed, but at a slower rate of 25 frames per second.

961 Give it some room

Another effect of the differing television standards around the world is that the safe area of the screen changes. The safe area is the part in which any titles, captions, or action will definitely be shown. Anything outside the safe area runs the risk of being cropped out by the TV. If you're authoring a DVD, go into preferences and select Show Safe Area, then set it to whichever standard is relevant. This will place guidelines on the screen, inside which menu buttons and suchlike can be safely placed.

Exporting video to DV tape

As we've seen in the earlier chapters on editing, all non-linear editing programs allow you to export the final cut of your video back to tape. Tape may seem old hat in these days of DVD and Internet video but, as widespread formats, DV or VHS tape offer almost everyone an easy way to watch your video.

962 Rendering your project

Most NLE systems offer you a real time preview of effects and transitions so that you can see what you're working on, but these previews won't transfer to tape. In order to get all the wipes, effects, and titles in your project onto tape, you have to render them. With your project on the timeline, click the Render All option and the computer will finalize all the effects ready for export.

963 Save to hard drive

Some older NLE systems won't allow you to export directly from their timeline and insist you save your edit as a video file prior to export. This is as easy as saving a word processor document—simply select Save Project As, pick a destination on your hard drive, and hit OK.

964 Crystal clear

Crystal Blacking is used to smooth the progress of transferring video from computer to tape by laying down a continuous data stream on the tape that can be followed by the export process. Put your final tape into the camcorder, put the lens cap on, and hit record until the tape runs out. The tape is now Blacked and ready to receive your video.

965 Choose a format and standard

Modern NLE systems provide all sorts of options for tape formats and video standards, and it's important to pick the right one. If you're exporting to DV, select DV not DV cam. If your tape is going to be sent overseas, find out what standard is used at the tape's destination and select it as your export option.

966 Set a pre roll

Pre roll is the amount of time the tape is rolling for before recording starts. Pre roll allows the tape transport mechanism to get up to normal speed and past the blank leader tape so that the start of your video isn't distorted or cut off. In the box for pre roll select at least eight seconds delay prior to recording.

967 Select an abort level

If you're using an older, slower computer, or are exporting from a slow hard drive (one that spins at around 5,200 RPM or slower) there is the possibility that it won't be able to keep up with the export process and will drop frames. This means losing video on the way to the tape. Too many dropped frames will be noticeable on your video, so the computer offers you the option to abort the transfer after a certain number of frames have been dropped. Any more than one or two dropped frames suggests a problem that needs fixing, so set the abort number quite low, or even at just one.

968 Export

Having set the export options, hit the export button and the computer will take control of your camcorder and begin transferring the video. This process will take fractionally longer than the duration of your video.

Exporting from DV to VHS

969 Old-Fashioned Formats

VHS is an even more widespread format than DV, and even though it has much lower picture quality it does offer your film a very big audience. Transferring DV to VHS is a simple process. First, follow the process just detailed to get your video onto a DV tape in your camcorder.

971 S-Video

For higher quality you can hook your camcorder's S-Video output to the VCR's S-Video input. S-Video processes color and brightness (chrominance and luminance) signals separately for better quality but isn't available on all camcorders and VCRs.

970 Connect your camcorder and VCR

You can connect your camcorder to your VCR in three ways. The most common method is to use the AV connection cable that comes with your camcorder, this is the cable with the 3.5mm jack at one end and the red, white (audio), and yellow (video) connectors at the other. These connectors can be plugged into the correspondingly colored socket on the back of your VCR, or into a SCART adaptor (also supplied with your camcorder) which is then plugged into the SCART socket on your VCR. This is the most commonly used connection as all VCRs have AV inputs and most have a 21-pin SCART socket.

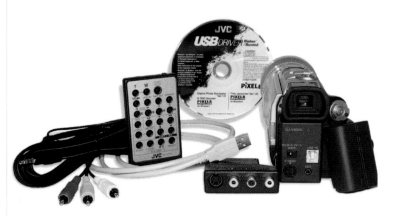

972 Moving with the times

In an attempt to stave off obsolescence, some VCRs now feature a DV input and can convert an incoming DV signal for recording to analog VHS tape. This is the best option of all, if your VCR is capable of it.

973 Hit it

Once your camcorder is connected to your VCR by one of the methods above, dubbing across is as easy as recording from the television. Simply press play on your camcorder and record on your VCR. Unlike DV tapes, there is no point in blacking a VHS tape as it won't hold a timecode.

Make A VCD or DVD

974 What's an MPEG?

MPEG stands for Motion Picture Experts Group, and put simply it's a type of compression. That is, all the masses of data that make up a video is squashed down to a size that fits onto a disc, hopefully with as little loss of quality as possible. DVDs use a version called MPEG2. VCDs use a lower quality called MPEG or MPEG1. There's even a sort of middle ground called MPEG4 which is good for making videos that can be posted on Web sites or in emails.

975 How does it work?

All video-editing programs have in them a codec (compressor/decompressor). When you choose MPEG or MPEG2 in your export settings box the codec takes every frame of video and identifies what has changed between frames. If you have a sequence with a tree and roadside in the foreground, and a car moving past in the background, the codec knows that it doesn't need to save all the information that relates to the foreground, just the stuff that relates to the car in the background. So, the more movement there is, the harder the codec has to work.

976 What is a bitrate?

Your codec is taking your video and squashing it down to a manageable size by ignoring anything that doesn't change from frame to frame. However, when there's a lot of movement, that means a lot of changes, so the codec has less to discard and more to keep. That's where bitrates come in. The bitrate is the amount of information contained in a second of video. If you set a high bitrate, then your video quality will be higher, as the codec will store more information about the changes and keep track of them better, but this will mean that the file size will be larger as more information is retained. That's the game with compression: balancing the quality of the video against the capacity of the disc.

977 VCD and SVCD

VCD (Video Compact Disc) and its flashier big brother SVCD (SuperVCD) are similar to DVD in as much as they consist of video files compressed into MPEG and burnt onto a disc. The major difference is that they are written to CD rather than DVD, resulting in much heavier compression in order to fit onto the lower-capacity discs. For this, they use MPEG rather than MPEG2.

978 Quality and compatibility

VCDs are of similar picture quality to VHS but have the advantage of being cheaper to produce, playable in computers and many DVD players, and easier to mail to far-off people. Another advantage is that VCDs can be produced using a CD Burner and either CD creation or NLE software, whereas DVDs require you to splash out on more expensive DVD-creation software and hardware. However, it's worth noting that not all DVD players can handle VCD. Strangely, it's usually the cheaper players that are sold in markets all around the world that are designed with broad compatibility in mind, so if you want to play VCDs it's usually a good idea to buy a cheap and cheerful DVD player.

979 Pick a program

Your options for creating VCDs are very broad indeed. If you are a Windows-user you'll find that almost every NLE program has a "create VCD" option in the export menu. If you use Apple editing software you'll find that only DVD creation is supported. However, products such as Roxio's Toast are inexpensive and offer a VCD option. You can even search the Web for VCD Creation Freeware and find plenty of totally free programs for compressing and burning video files from your hard drive to VCD. VCD creation involves compressing the video very carefully, due to the massive reduction in data rate. There is little margin for error, which actually makes things easier for beginners, as your VCD creation template will, of necessity, be forced to do all the work rather than leaving it in your hands. VCD creation therefore tends to be a one-step process.

981 DVD, Blu-Ray, HD-DVD

DVD-R and DVD+R are two long-established, competing versions of the same format, but both will play in a standard home player. Rewriteable versions (DVD-RW and DVD+RW) are also available. Two emerging formats are Blu-Ray and HD-DVD. Both offer vastly superior, multi-gigabyte storage capacities, but hardware for each format is not yet compatible with the other, so choose carefully. Both new formats require special players/recorders, as data is written using blue lasers rather than the standard red.

980 Make a DVD

DVD is the most successful home entertainment technology ever, in terms of the speed of its market penetration. Just about everyone now has a DVD player, meaning that DVD is an excellent way to share your videos. The exact terms used by the various authoring programs vary, but the procedure for making a DVD remains the same.

982 The write tools for the job

There are two methods for creating your own DVDs from a DV tape, the first is a FireWire-equipped DVD recorder, the second is a DVD burner in your computer.

983 The easy way

The easiest method is to use a DVD recorder with a FireWire input. Like VCRs, DVD recorders are essentially DVD players that can also be used to record from TV. If, however, you get one equipped with a FireWire port, you can simply plug in your camcorder and hit record just like you would with VHS. This is the easiest method of putting your work on DVD, but it lacks the flexibility and creative control provided by a burner.

984 Feel the burn

Using a burner built into your computer is the best way of creating a DVD similar to the ones you buy in the shops. You get to have a moving menu background, buttons, multiple scenes, even surround sound audio, and subtitles if you have an advanced authoring program. To create a DVD this way, all you need is a burner built into your computer, which is commonplace these days, and an authoring package that will let you design the menus and encode the video.

985 Author, author!

Authoring is the term used for creating a playable MPEG of your video and designing a menu that will work with it. Authoring packages range from the free ones that come installed on your computer, such as Apple's iDVD and Sony's ClickToDVD, through to inexpensive beginners' programs that guide you through the process step by step, such as Ulead's DVD Workshop, all the way up to the sort of programs that will let you create surround sound, manage multiple angles, and create subtitles and special features, such as Apple's DVD Studio Pro or Adobe Encore.

986 A new chapter

Chapter points are a common feature on shop-bought DVDs and can also be a feature on your homemade ones. Editing packages allow you to create chapter markers in your video before you even open it with your authoring program. Simply play through the timeline, stop the playhead where you want a chapter point to be, then hit the add chapter marker in the Markers menu.

987 To put it another way

You can also add chapter markers within your authoring program. Your first step is to click the File menu and select Import or Get Video, which will bring your DV footage from your hard drive into the authoring program. Then you can drag the footage into the preview window, play it, and hit the space bar to mark your chapter points.

988 What's on the menu?

Next you have to choose a menu background. All DVD authoring programs come with a selection of themed templates that you can use as the background onto which you place all your buttons. These can be customized by changing the text to something relevant, and by adding pictures and sometimes moving video loops.

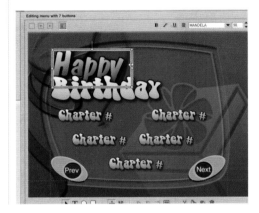

990 Margin of error

Hopefully, your authoring program will have safe area guides that will show you which part of your menus will be safely displayed on any TV set. If it doesn't, a simple rule of thumb is to imagine a danger area of 10 percent around the edge of the screen like a border–this is the area where buttons or graphics risk being cropped. Try not to place anything in it.

991 Customize your buttons

Now that your buttons are placed and have video attached, you can customize them. By double-clicking the text that says Button1 you can highlight it and type a more descriptive title. By double-clicking the button itself, you'll be presented with a slider that will allow you to skim through the video attached to the button until you find a fitting frame of video to be displayed in the button.

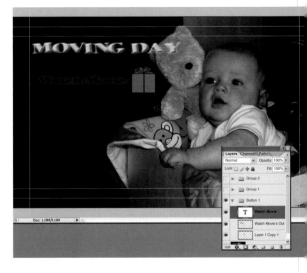

989 Add buttons

Your authoring program will have provided some ready-made buttons on the template, and will have a button marked Add Button which you can click to create more controls on your menu. Once your buttons are on the menu background, you add video to them simply by clicking on the relevant video file in the browser and dragging onto the correct button.

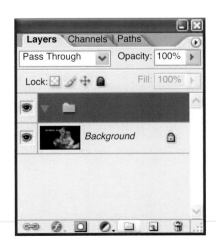

992 Preview mode

When you think your menu is finished, hit the preview button. This brings up an imitation DVD remote control with all the buttons you'd find on the real thing. Use this to navigate around your disc in the same way your audience would. Do all the buttons work? Do they all link to something? Does the menu structure make sense? If you can say yes to all these questions, you're ready to burn the disc.

994 QuickTime

There are three main tools for creating and playing Web and email video: QuickTime, RealPlayer, and Windows Media Player. In the export options box of your video-editing software you'll be presented with choices for one, two, or all three, depending on the program you use. QuickTime is Apple's media player, although, like all three, there are versions available for all computer platforms. The in-built QuickTime codec, H.264, is specifically designed with web video in mind, although all three players are primarily used for Web video, so are suitable for the purpose.

995 RealPlayer

RealPlayer is platform-independent and has to be downloaded rather than coming supplied with your computer. It benefits from regular upgrades, but be warned, it can occasionally cause problems on older machines, and the regular upgrades that keep it cutting edge also mean that older versions of the player frequently become obsolete.

993 Going online

Putting your video online is the most popular way of making sure anyone can see it, although it does involve drastically reducing the image size and quality. But that's a small price to pay for making your video accessible to the whole world. You can prepare video for the Web from inside your editing software, and host it on your own Web site, or a specialist site such as Google's Video Blog, Mydeo.com, or Atomfilms.com.

996 Windows Media Player

Thanks to the near ubiquity of Windows-based computers, Windows Media files are the ones most likely to be compatible with the broadest audience possible.

997 Screen size

Having chosen what type of file to make, you need to choose a screen size. Reducing the screen size helps make the file size smaller. With broadband connections being commonplace these days, you don't need to shrink the picture down to postage-stamp size, but a reasonable size reduction will cater for both broadband and dial-up users. Selecting 320 x 240 in the options list is ideal. Alternatively, you could make multiple versions in order to cater for all connection types.

998 Frame rate

By reducing the frame rate you massively decrease the number of individual images the codec needs to compress, although you simultaneously make the video jumpier, as the "persistence of vision" effect upon which video works is decreased. A good middle ground is about 15fps. This will be noticeably less smooth than ordinary video, but not disruptively so.

999 Audio

Even though you can't see sound, it still takes up space in your video file. Unless it's vital that you have stereo audio, we'd suggest you select mono audio in the encode settings box, as this will save on file size without wrecking the sound.

1000 Encode

Having chosen all your encode preferences, you can hit the save button and the codec will begin creating the video to your specifications. This may take a while depending on the length of your video, but by the time you're finished you'll have what this whole book has been leading up to–a great video that can be shared with anyone, anywhere in the world.

Glossary

AE
Automatic Exposure. When the camera automatically sets shutter speed and aperture value, precise control over depth of field and movement cannot be guaranteed.

AF
Auto-focus or automatic focus. With this system, most compact cameras lock focus on the object in the center of the frame, which can cause a problem if composition is off-center. Better SLRs have multizone autofocus systems, which can respond to more creative framing. Autofocus works best when locked onto an area with sufficient contrast.

Aperture
The hole in the lens through which light passes en route to the film. Each aperture is given an f/number to denote its size. Large apertures have a small f/number, such as f/2.8; small apertures have a large f/number, like f/16.

Aperture-priority function
Automatic exposure mode, where the photographer defines the aperture value and the camera automatically sets the appropriate shutter speed for correct exposure.

Audio dub
Some camcorders allow you to leave an audio track free so that you can dub extra audio onto our footage later without disturbing the original sound.

Bit
A bit is the smallest piece of computer data, namely one binary digit ("bit" is short for "binary digit"). Binary code deals with calculations in long streams of invisible 1s and 0s, which is all a computer's onboard microchip is processing. More information can be stored in longer strings, so 24-bit systems or files contain more detailed information than 16-bit, for example.

Blurring
Blurred images are frequently caused by unsteady hands moving the camera slightly during long exposures. The problem is more noticeable in low-light situations, but is easily overcome using a tripod to hold the camera steady while the shutter is open. Always use at least 1/250 second or 1/125 second exposures with long telephoto lenses.

Burning
A processing technique in which specific areas of the image are made lighter, for artistic effect.

Burst rate
The number of images that can be recorded in succession by a digital camera.

Calibration
The process of matching characteristics or behavior of a device to a standard to ensure accuracy.

Catch light
The reflections created by highlights or bright objects that appear in your subject's eyes and make them look more lively.

CCD
Charge coupled device. This is one type of light-sensitive sensor used in place of film in a digital camera. A CCD is like a honeycomb of tiny individual cells, with each one creating an individual pixel.

CF card
CompactFlash memory card. A small, removable card on which can be stored up to one or more gigabytes of data, depending on the card's capacity.

Channels
The method that Photoshop and other image-editing software use to manage color, by separating them into separate editable channels. (See also CMYK, LAB, and RGB).

CMYK
Cyan, magenta, yellow, and black. The color management system used in commercial printing, whereby colors are formed using combinations of these four inks. In Photoshop, you can choose to edit images for print in CMYK mode, which Photoshop uses to separate an image into four editable color channels. (See also Channels, LAB, and RGB).

Codec
An abbreviation of compressor/decompressor: a tool for reducing the file size of video by compression. Codecs use algorithms to discard certain data and save only the important changes. These algorithms are later used to reconstitute the image. Codecs can be either hardware of software.

Color cast
A wash of color that can appear on digital images, especially on areas that should be white, and usually when the image has been shot under artificial light. The problem can be overcome using White Balance controls (see White Balance).

Color temperature
An exact measurement of light color, expressed using the Kelvin (K) scale.

Compression
The act of reducing the size of a digital file by losing some detail, while attempting to retain as much of the original detail and quality as possible. Compression methods can be "lossless" (little visible detail is lost) or "lossy" (there is a noticeable degrading of image quality).

Continuous shooting (mode)
Camera mode that allows you to shoot a series of images in quick succession. The speed of the mode depends on the quality at which you are shooting as higher-resolution images require much more processing time.

Contrast
The difference in brightness between the highlights and shadows in a scene. When that difference is great, contrast is high; when it is small, contrast is low.

Converging verticals
A problem common in architectural photography that makes buildings appear to be toppling over, caused when the camera is tilted to include the top of a structure.

Cropping

Images can be recomposed after shooting by a process called cropping. Digital photographers can use the Crop tool in image-editing software packages to remove unwanted pixels.

CRT Screen

Cathode Ray Tube, the standard type of computer monitor now being increasingly replaced by flat plasma screens and LCD technologies.

CSR

Continuous shooting rate—the number of images that can be taken before the shutter delay locks to enable processing to take place.

Density

The measure of darkness, blackening, or "strength" of an image in terms of its ability to stop light (this is also referred to as its opacity).

Depth of field

The zone of sharpness set between the nearest and farthest points of a scene. It is controlled by two factors: your position relative to the subject, and the aperture value. Higher f-numbers, such as f/22, create a greater depth of field than lower numbers, such as f/2.8.

Dodging

A technique in which specific areas of the image are made lighter, for artistic effect.

Exposure

The act of opening the shutter to allow light to fall onto the sensor via the lens to record a scene. A fast or slow exposure describes the length of time the shutter remains open and the sensor is exposed to the light (see also overexposure and underexposure).

Fast lenses

Lenses with a wide maximum aperture, such as 300mm f/2.8 or a 50mm f/1.4.

Fill-flash

The camera's built-in flash.

Filters

In all photography, glass, plastic, or gelatin filters can be attached to a camera lens for adding different creative effects to a photograph. Filters work by absorbing or allowing through different wavelengths of light, thereby enabling some colors to pass through to the film while others are prevented from doing so.

Flare

Nonimage-forming light that reduces image quality by lowering contrast and washing out colors.

Flash

An onboard or external light source for photography which produces a short burst, rather than a continuous source, of light that is calibrated to be of a consistent and neutral color.

Flatten

In Photoshop and other layer-based image-editing programs, the process of compiling all of an image's separate layers into a single layer containing all of the image information. Once flattened, edits can no longer be made in isolation to information that previously resided on a separate layer.

F-number

Aperture numbers are described in terms of their f-numbers, such as f/2.8 and f/1.6. Smaller f-numbers let more light into the camera, and bigger f-numbers, less light.

Focal length

The distance between the near nodal point of the lens and the film plane when the lens is focused on infinity also used to express a lens' optical power.

Focal point

The point where light rays meet after passing through the lens to give a sharp image. Also used to describe the most important element in a picture.

FPS

Frames per second—the number of images that can be recorded by a digital camera within a one-second period.

GIF

Graphics Interchange Format. A universal image format designed for monitor and network use only. Not suitable for saving photographic images due to the 256-color, 8-bit palette.

Gigabyte (GB)

A unit expressing digital file size or memory capacity. One gigabyte equals one thousand megabytes.

Grain

The gritty texture characteristic of fast films, which can be imitated digitally in Photoshop and other image-editing programs to create a variety of effects. Fast films have a larger amount of light-sensitive silver halide crystals, which are often visible as texture in the final image.

Graphics tablet

An input device that works like a pen on a pad, to be used in image processing.

Grayscale

In digital imaging, the grayscale mode is used to create and save black and white images. In a standard 8-bit Grayscale there are 256 steps from black to white, just enough to prevent banding visible to the human eye.

HD (High-definition)

A video format of very high quality. Often touted as a potential replacement for film.

HDD

The hard-disk drive on a computer that serves as a computer's filing cabinet, also known as the hard disk.

High resolution

High-resolution images are generally captured with many millions of pixels and are used to make high-quality printouts.

Histogram
A graphic representation of tonal range in an image.

Hyperfocal distance
A focus setting used to give maximum depth of field.

Interface
The way in which a peripheral (such as a scanner) links to the computer.

Interpolate
The way in which a digital camera calculates a color value for each pixel.

ISO/ISO-E
International Standards Organization. The ISO standard describes film and DPS speed. In film photography, the ISO value describes a film's ability to work under low or bright light conditions. For example, ISO 100 is a slow film suitable for the brightest light situations, ISO 200 and 400 are general-purpose films, while ISO 800, 1600, and above are for shooting in lowest light conditions. Digital cameras use the same system to describe ISO equivalency (ISO-EO. Just like aperture and shutter speed scales, the doubling or halving of an ISO value halves and doubles the amount of light needed to make a successful exposure.

JPEG
Joint Photographic Experts Group—a file format for saving images to memory, which reduces file size.

Jump cut
A noticeable change in framing or perspective between two edits, causing the subject to appear to "jump" from one position to another. Usually considered a mistake, but often used for dramatic effect.

Keyframe
One of a series of marked frames in a video that allows for complicated effects to be simplified. By marking the state of the effect at certain keyframes, the effects software can be left to figure out what comes in-between.

Layer
In Photoshop and some other programs, each new element of, or amendment to, an image is (or can be) made on a separate, individually editable layer, as though it were on an invisible overlay. In this way all editing is non-destructive of the original image, giving you an extremely high level of control over each element.

Lens hood
An accessory used to shade the front element of your lenses from stray light so reducing the risk of flare.

Linear editing
The process of assembling a film by copying shots to tape sequentially.

Macro
A term used to describe close-up photography. The lens itself determines how close you can focus and not all cameras are fitted with macro lenses as standard. Many mid-range zoom lenses offer an additional macro function, but much better results are gained by using specially designed macro lenses. When close focusing, effective depth of field shrinks to a matter of centimeters even when using narrow apertures like f/22.

Megabyte (MB)
Megabytes—units of memory or hard disk space on a computer.

Megapixel
A measurement of the maximum bitmap size a digital camera can create. A bitmap image measuring 1800 x 1200 pixels contains 2.1 million pixels (1800 x 1200 = 2.1 million), the maximum capture size of a 2.1 Megapixel camera. The higher the megapixel number, the bigger and better quality print out you can make.

Mirror lock-up
A device found in some cameras that allows you to lock up the reflex mirror prior to taking a picture to reduce vibrations and the risk of camera shake.

Monochromatic
This means "one color" and is often used to describe black-and-white photography or color photography when an image comprises different shades of the same color.

MPEG
A compression standard for moving images, named after the Motion (or Moving) Picture Experts Group. Works by storing critical frames and the differences between them as opposed to the full footage. Variations include MPEG1 (a lower quality compression used in VCDs), MPEG4 (used for email video), and MPEG2 (used on DVDs). The compressed audio format MP3 is derived from MPEG.

NLE (Non-linear Editing)
The process of using a computer or "one box editor" to construct a video from footage saved to hard disk. Because non-linear editing doesn't involve working with the original material it is non-destructive, allowing you to work in any order you wish before saving the completed project and sending it back to tape or disk.

Noise
Electronic disturbances that affect the quality of the photographic image, also known as digital grain.

NR
Noise reduction. In photography, a method of removing unwanted image artifacts (see Artifacts, Noise).

NTSC (National Television System Committee)
Television system of 525 lines used mainly in the US, Canada, South America, and parts of the Caribbean.

Overexposure
The act of allowing light to fall on the sensor (or film, in film photography) for too long, resulting in images that are pale and washed out (overexposed).

PAL (Phase Alternating Line)

A television standard of 625 lines at 25fps used in many parts of the world, including the UK, much of Western Europe, parts of Asia, and Australia.

Panning

A technique where the camera is moved during the exposure to keep the subject sharp but blurring the background.

Panorama

A single image stitched together from several separate images shot from a tripod that is gradually rotated through 360 degrees.

Photomerge

Application for stitching together images to form a single panoramic shot.

Pixels

The elements that make up a digital image.

Prime lens

Any lens with a fixed focal length, such as 28mm, 50mm, or 300mm.

RAW (raw)

A type of picture file that takes data directly off the digital sensor for storing on the memory device.

Red eye

A familiar image anomaly that occurs when direct on-camera flash is used when photographing someone at close range, caused by the flash bouncing off the retina and being recorded as a disk of red, most cameras have a red-eye reduction mode, which works by firing a swift succession of strobe-like flashes that close down the subject's iris before the shutter fires.

Rendering

The process of your computer working out all the changes made to a piece of video by an effect and applying them. Faster processors render more quickly, and certain capture cards include separate processors for handling rendering.

Resolution

An often confusing concept. Very broadly speaking, a high-resolution image is one that contains the highest number of pixels (picture elements), or dots of light, resulting in a more finely detailed recording of a scene. Of printing and computer monitor displays, resolution refers to the number of elements (dots of ink, or dots of light) needed to reproduce an image accurately. Computer monitors have a much lower resolution (72 dots per inch) than printed matter (300 or more dots per inch). Therefore, an image saved down to Web resolution can appear sharp and detailed onscreen, but seem very poor quality when printed. (In this way, file sizes can be kept as small as possible for posting images online for quick download.)

Rule of thirds

A compositional formula used to place the focal point of a shoot a third into the frame for visual balance.

Sharpen

In Photoshop and other image-editing software, you can use one or more of the various Sharpen tools to increase the contrast between pixels on the edges of objects within an image, creating the impression of a sharper, more detailed shot. Sharpening will not compensate for an out-of-focus image, however. All digital images require slight sharpening, which can be done in-camera.

Shutter-priority function

Automatic exposure mode, where the user sets the shutter speed and the camera automatically sets the appropriate aperture for correct exposure—also known as shutter priority auto exposure.

SLR

Single Lens Reflex camera. A type of camera that allows you to see through the camera's lens as you look through the viewfinder.

Stitching

The process of using image-editing software to join together a series of separate images into a single image, usually to create a panorama. Images are shot with a slight overlap so that the stitching software can find the correct join.

Stop

The term used to describe on f/stop. If you "close down" a stop you select the next smallest aperture; if you "open-up" a stop you select the next largest aperture.

Teleconverter

An alternative to a telephoto lens, used to increase the effective focal length of the camera's lens.

Telephoto

A lens with a long or very long focal length, which lets in the least amount of a subject (the opposite of a wideangle lens), and is useful for focusing on distant objects and keeping vertical lines perpendicular.

TIFF

Tag Image File Format, the most common cross-platform image format. Compressed TIFFs use a lossless routine to retain image data.

TTL metering

Through the lens metering—a system of light metering that measures the amount of light reflected through the lens.

Underexposure

The act of allowing light to fall on the sensor for too short a time, resulting in images that are muddy, dark, and poorly detailed (underexposed).

WB

White balance—a camera setting that overcomes color shifts caused by the different color temperatures of light.

Wildtrack

Sound recorded independently from the pictures for later dubbing.

Index

Author biographies

Philip Andrews is an experienced photographer, author, magazine editor, and online course creator. He is Adobe Australia's official Photoshop and Elements Ambassador. Philip is a cofounder of photo-college.com, an online training college, and is a regular contributor to several photography magazines.

Lee Frost is a professional landscape and travel photographer. He is the author of several photography books and is a regular contributor to photography magazines.

Robert Hull is the editor of *Digital Video Magazine*, and former editor of *Camcorder User*. Jamie Ewbank is the deputy editor of *Digital Video Magazine*.

Chris Weston is a professional photographer and also writes regularly for the photographic press. He is the author of over twenty books, including *Mastering Your Digital SLR*, *The Essential Lighting Manual*, and *Mastering Digital Exposure and HDR Imaging*.